"SHOULD I BUY OR LEASE?"

Money® magazine knows that buying a car isn't what it used to be: it's more expensive, more complicated, and more daunting than ever before. Now Money® brings together in one book the answers to the questions car buyers ask most:

- On my budget, how much car can I really afford?
- Are car-shopping services really worth the fee?
- What is the best way to finance a car?
- How can I be sure repair costs are covered by warranty?
- What is my old car worth?

Car Shopping Made Easy

Money® magazine

Other books in the
Money® America's Financial Advisor series:

How to Retire Young and Rich

401(k) Take Charge of Your Life

Paying for Your Child's College Education

The Right Way to Invest in Mutual Funds

Dollar Pinching: A Consumer's Guide to Smart Spending

Starting Over: How to Change Careers or Start Your Own Business

Car Shopping Made Easy

Buying or Leasing, New or Used

Jerry Edgerton

WARNER BOOKS

A Time Warner Company

A NOTE FROM THE PUBLISHER

This publication is designed to provide competent and reliable information regarding the subject matter covered. However, it is sold with the understanding that the author and publisher are not engaged in rendering legal, financial, or other professional advice. Laws and practices often vary from state to state and if legal or other expert assistance is required, the services of a professional should be sought. The author and publisher specifically disclaim any liability that is incurred from the use or application of the contents of this book.

Copyright © 1997 by MONEY magazine
All rights reserved.

Warner Books, Inc., 1271 Avenue of the Americas, New York, NY 10020
Visit our Web site at
http://pathfinder.com/twep

 A Time Warner Company

Printed in the United States of America
First Printing: March 1997
10 9 8 7 6 5 4 3 2 1

Library of Congress Cataloging-in-Publication Data
Edgerton, Jerry.
    Car shopping made easy : buying or leasing, new or used / Jerry Edgerton.
      p. cm.
    Includes index.
    ISBN 0-446-67244-0
    1. Automobiles—Purchasing. 2. Automobile leasing and renting.
I. Title.
TL162.E314   1997
629.222'029'6—dc20   96-34867
                                      CIP

Book design and text composition by L & G McRee
Cover design by Bernadette Evangelist © by Robert Anthony, Inc.
Cover illustration by Peter Hoey

For Lynn, My Favorite Wordsmith

ACKNOWLEDGMENTS

Thanks to my auto industry sources who made extra efforts with information for this book, especially Ashly Knapp of AutoAdvisor, Art Spinella of CNW Marketing/Research, Charles Hart of Chart Software, and the J.D. Power organization.

Thanks also to Jillian Kasky for her computer and logistical support.

CONTENTS

INTRODUCTION
Answering Crucial Car Questions 1

PART 1
CHOOSING THE RIGHT VEHICLE FOR YOUR LIFE AND YOUR BUDGET 5

CHAPTER 1
The Car You Want, the Car You Need: Getting It Right 7

CHAPTER 2
Your Auto-Biography: The Right Car or Truck for the Job 20

CHAPTER 3
Staying Safe, Saving Money 30

CONTENTS

CHAPTER 4

Your Answers, Your Deal 43

CHAPTER 5

What Can You Afford? Don't Kid Yourself 53

CHAPTER 6

Getting the Lowdown and Setting Your Price 64

CHAPTER 7

Shopping for Money 76

PART 2

SHOPPING FOR THE BEST DEAL 85

CHAPTER 8

**Hate Haggling? Then Hire Help: Buying Services Can Help
You Get the Best Prices with Little Hassle 87**

CHAPTER 9

One Price but Not the Highest Price 97

CHAPTER 10

Leasing: Through the Looking Glass 103

CHAPTER 11

**Scoping out Service: Finding the Right Dealer to Work
on Your Car 116**

CHAPTER 12

**Getting Down to the Deal: How to Negotiate with
Confidence and Get the Best Price 123**

CONTENTS

CHAPTER 13
**Closing the Deal: Making Sure You Don't Sign away
the Savings You Just Negotiated 133**

CHAPTER 14
Buying a Used Car: Getting the Most Car for the Least 138

CHAPTER 15
Got a Lemon? Don't Let It Squeeze You 154

CHAPTER 16
**Down the Road: Mechanical Maintenance and
Financial Planning 159**

CHAPTER 17
Summing up: Step by Step to a Great Deal 162

GLOSSARY 165

APPENDIX A
**Insurance Costs: How Cars, Trucks, Vans, and Utilities
Stack Up 169**

APPENDIX B
Record of Injuries 179

APPENDIX C
Rating the Crash Tests 189

APPENDIX D
How Much Loan for the Payments 193

INDEX 197

Car Shopping Made Easy

INTRODUCTION

Answering Crucial
Car Questions

Maybe it was the third time in as many months that the engine of your old clunker overheated. Or the moment your 16-year-old finally got her driver's license, letting you hang up your chauffeur's hat at last. Or even the amazing day that miserly Aunt Minnie died and bequeathed you her modest nest egg. Whatever the occasion, it motivated you to make a major decision: you are ready to get yourself another car.

That doesn't mean, however, that you're also ready to rush to a nearby car dealer. These days you need to make informed choices about not only what car, truck, van, or sport utility to buy, but also where, when, and how to pay for it. If you don't do your homework, you run a real risk of getting the wrong car at the wrong price. And that is a very expensive mistake—now that the average price for new cars is about $18,500. Since 1979 that figure has soared 167%, while median family income has risen just 113%. As a result, manufacturers are constantly coming up with new gimmicks to make cars seem more affordable.

But you don't want to—and you don't have to—take their

word for it. In Part 1 of this book we will show you how to figure out precisely what car or truck you want, what vehicle you can afford, plus how to calculate the deal you need to make. In Part 2, we demonstrate just how to nail down that deal—complete with negotiating scripts so even the most silver-tongued sales folk cannot sway you from the price you plan to pay. If you prefer, we will tell you how to hire someone to do that negotiating for you.

Along the way, this book will help you explore—and answer—crucial questions with our questionnaires, worksheets, and clarifying charts and tables. We will give you the kind of accurate, authoritative data and advice you have come to expect from **MONEY** magazine. Some of the key questions:

- Should I buy or lease?
- Is a new car or used car best for me?
- What is my old car worth?
- What car really suits my lifestyle?
- What can I actually afford?
- If I do a lot of family driving, do I have to buy a minivan?
- Where do I go for reliable information about prices?
- Does the dealer's cost matter? Where can I find it?
- How do I determine what price I intend to pay?
- What hidden costs can raise my insurance?
- How does safety pay for itself?
- In what cars and trucks do passengers sustain the fewest injuries?
- What vehicles are most and least likely to be stolen?
- How can I test-drive the vehicles that interest me most?
- If I can pay cash for a car, is that likely to be the best deal?
- Where and how do I shop for the best auto loan?
- How can I tell if a lease deal is a good one or just a come-on with low payments?
- Will I get a decent deal at a "one-price" dealer, where there is no haggling?

- Do I want to avoid car dealers entirely and hire someone to do the car shopping for me?

Buying a car does not have to be as brutal as a game of Mortal Kombat. It is a challenge, not a war. If you buy or lease the car, truck, sport utility, or van you really want and do it for the price you had budgeted and planned to pay, then you can relax and enjoy your new wheels, knowing you got a good deal.

PART 1

CHOOSING THE RIGHT VEHICLE FOR YOUR LIFE AND YOUR BUDGET

CHAPTER 1

The Car You Want, the Car You Need: Getting It Right

Admit it: we've all fallen for the wrong stuff on occasion. Maybe it was those blue jeans that won't fit unless you inhale and stand at attention. Or perhaps it was that supremely ugly lamp that somehow looked beguiling in the store.

Such mistakes don't cost much and are easy to rectify; why else would God have invented yard sales? But when you're talking about nearly $20,000—enough to send one of your kids through at least a couple of years at State U—a wrong decision can inflict some serious damage.

Yet time and again shoppers leap into a car or truck purchase without first considering carefully what vehicle is really right for them. Sure, you know you don't want your father's Oldsmobile, but why opt so quickly for your boss's BMW, your sister's Saturn, or your lawyer's Lexus? Maybe you craved a Corvette as a teenager, but now that you finally can afford one, does it still really represent your heart's desire? Just because every other mom in your suburb drives a minivan, does that mean you need one?

The way vehicles are advertised and sold can add to your

7

confusion. "We try to design cars that appeal to the customer's emotion as well as intellect," declared Chrysler chairman Robert Eaton in a recent speech. Nothing wrong with that, as long as you make sure *you* always know the difference and evaluate both aspects. To do so, you need to prepare your own auto-biography—an accurate picture of the car, truck, van, or sport utility that meets the demands of your lifestyle, livelihood, and pocketbook.

Don't ignore the psychological side. Your ideal vehicle should make you smile—or at least not wince—when it sits in the driveway as well as when you are tooling down the road. And the best bargain in your neighborhood will not look so special six months later if you hate the car it bought you. For instance, after weighing all his options, one New Yorker we know decided that he would rather buy a used Mercedes than a new Plymouth Neon because a Mercedes—even an old one—made him feel pampered.

Remember the Batmobile

Be sure, though, to measure your dream car against the demands of life as you really live it. Batman's Batmobile suits him because not only is it a knockout, it also works perfectly on crime-fighting forays. As you consider vehicles, be especially careful not to get a case of the might-go's. Should you find yourself thinking, "If I had a sport utility I might go hiking a lot," when in fact you have not been hiking in the past five years, sound the fantasy alert and cross that off as a worthy reason for choosing a certain vehicle. Reflect on what you actually do when gazing into your automotive future. If you tell yourself, "With a van, we could put those antiques and gardening supplies we are always buying into the back immediately instead of needing to have them delivered," that can be a valid consideration.

Ask a Frank Friend

To test your vision of yourself in a specific car, truck, or van, talk to your friends and relatives before you decide what to buy—rather than just turning up later with a new vehicle to show them. "The question to ask is not what do your friends think of a specific car or truck—ask them what they think of *you* in that vehicle," says Ashly Knapp, president of Seattle-based car-buying service AutoAdvisor, which sometimes finds itself dealing with clients who bought the wrong vehicle the last time. If you're deluding yourself, a friend who knows you well could pipe up with: "Why are you going to buy that sporty two-door coupe when you always have three or four people in your car? Who has to climb into the backseat?" Good question.

Do Sweat the Details

Even seemingly small details can loom large when they interfere with your everyday use of the car. That is just what Kathy Rossi, a transportation planner in Seattle, learned to her cost and chagrin. Her 1985 Toyota Camry did not provide enough room for her two children, eight and 11, and their bikes. She went shopping and saw a 1991 Colt Vista Wagon—a hybrid that is smaller than a sport utility but larger than a traditional station wagon. "The kids jumped in the back and said this is wonderful— just what we need," she recalls. Only one problem: the wagon had a manual transmission, and she always had driven automatic. "But after the salesman gave me a lesson in the parking lot, I decided this stick shift isn't bad," she recounts. She paid $7,850 for the four-year-old car.

Within three months Rossi decided she had made a terrible mistake. The flat parking lot was nothing like the hilly areas where she lives and does most of her driving. Navigating hills requires more frequent shifting. Rossi hated it. So she went shopping again—this time without the kids—and moved up to a 1992 Mitsubishi Expo—the same vehicle as the Colt Vista but with a different nameplate, under a cooperative arrangement between Chrysler and Mitsubishi. Rossi bargained the price for the Expo down to $12,250 and decided to sell the Vista herself instead of trading it in. But when she had trouble finding buyers through the classified ads who would pay the price she wanted, she wound up with two monthly car payments until she finally sold the Colt Vista. Her advice to other shoppers is, "Don't brush aside details about the car that bother you. And leave the kids at home when you shop. They can really sway you."

Rossi's extreme and unusual situation emphasizes yet another critical point—affordability. Don't stop counting with the monthly payments on your loan or lease. Insuring the car is a major item, and insurance costs can vary widely between two similar vehicles. Repairs, maintenance, and—if you're buying new—the eventual likely resale value of your choice all need to enter your calculations. (For detailed advice on working out what you can afford, see Chapter 5.) Perhaps the only thing worse than finding out you bought the wrong car is buying a vehicle that seems perfect and then discovering you can't really afford it.

Before you move on to decide what car you really need, here is a rundown of the categories of vehicles, their prices, and their advantages and drawbacks.

Small Cars

Description: Their low (by current standards) prices and high gas mileage may interest you if you are a budget-conscious buyer—either young and looking for your first new car or trying to buy an affordable second car for the family. Most of these short cars have a wheelbase (the distance between front and back wheels) of less than 100 inches.

Models: This class includes Dodge and Plymouth Neon, Ford Aspire, Ford Escort, Geo Metro, Geo Prizm, Mazda Protege, Mitsubishi Mirage, Saturn SC, Subaru Impreza, Toyota Corolla, Toyota Tercel, and Volkswagen Jetta.

Price: Almost always under $15,000 and frequently below $12,000.

Trends: Manufacturers once focused only on providing low price with these vehicles, but now have added more sophisticated technology for better handling and more comfortable rides.

Pluses: Mileage as rated by the Environmental Protection Agency, often above 25 MPG in city driving and 30 MPG on the highway, keeps the gas bills low to go with low monthly payments. With overall length usually less than 175 inches (14.6 feet), these cars fit the tightest urban parking spots.

Minuses: Cramped seating space and difficulty getting in and out often afflict rear seat riders. In most cases only front seat passengers enjoy a comfortable ride.

Midsize Cars

Description: With a wheelbase generally between 103 and 106 inches, these cars—except for the convertibles and two-door coupe models—have more room than small models for rear seat passengers and decent trunk space. If this is the only family vehicle and you can afford the difference, opt for a midsize over a small model. Gas mileage here runs to the low 20s for the city and the high 20s for highway driving.

Models: This class includes Buick Skylark, Chevrolet Cavalier,

Chevrolet Corsica, Chrysler Cirrus, Ford Contour, Ford Taurus, Honda Accord, Honda Civic, Hyundai Sonata, Mazda 626, Mitsubishi Galant, Nissan Altima, Nissan Maxima, Oldsmobile Achieva, Pontiac Grand AM, Saab 900, Saturn SL, Subaru Legacy, Toyota Camry, and Volkswagen Passat.

Price: The bulk of these models falls in the $15,000–$22,000 range, although with a full load of optional equipment, the priciest of them can reach $25,000.

Trends: Home to the biggest-selling cars like the Ford Taurus and Honda Accord, this segment is a prime battleground among the big Detroit and foreign car companies. Look for rebates or subsidized lease deals on slow-selling models.

Pluses: You get the most people- and cargo-hauling space for your money in this category, especially if you catch a rebate or otherwise get a good deal.

Minuses: Since these cars are big sellers, you will often see an exact replica of your car at the mall parking lot or the PTA meeting. That may not bother you. If you haul lots of people or cargo, these sedans can't measure up to a minivan for roominess.

Large Cars

Description: With wheelbases of 107 up to 115 inches, these sedans will interest you chiefly if you need real backseat room to haul people and a sizable trunk for things like luggage and golf clubs. Most of these cars can seat five and sometimes six people comfortably. With bigger engines, these cars range from 18 to19 MPG in city driving to about 24 MPG on the highway.

Models: This class includes Buick LeSabre, Chevrolet Lumina, Chevrolet Monte Carlo, Chrysler New Yorker, Dodge Intrepid, Ford Crown Victoria, Mazda Millenia, Mercury Grand Marquis, Oldsmobile Cutlass Supreme, Oldsmobile Eighty-Eight, Pontiac Bonneville, Pontiac Grand Prix, and Toyota Avalon.

Price: These prices range widely, with the biggest number of models falling in the $20,000–$28,000 range. But General Motors divisions—Buick, Chevrolet, Oldsmobile, and Pontiac—have low-end versions starting below $20,000.

Trends: Still engineered primarily for a comfortable ride, some of these large cars can also be fun to drive, unthinkable in big U.S. sedans until recent years.

Pluses: If you regularly haul colleagues or clients to lunch, meetings, or conferences, your passengers will thank you for the roominess in one of these cars.

Minuses: Your practicality will be admired, but almost no one will praise you for your sense of style with most of these cars.

Luxury Cars

Description: Large size meets style and cachet in this category, but you pay for the combination. With their leather seats, quiet ride, and heavily promoted trademarks, these cars say "I have both a roomy and a stylish car because I have the money to pay for it."

Models: Brand name is the key here. BMW, Mercedes-Benz, and Lexus probably are the top luxury lines today. Also fitting the luxury mold are Acura, Audi, Cadillac, Infiniti, Jaguar, and Lincoln. Volvo, while it has a bit more spartan image than the others and emphasizes safety in its ads, generally fits in here as well. Individual cars of a few other makers, such as the Oldsmobile Aurora and Buick Park Avenue, also compete with luxury brands.

Price: These cars start around $35,000 and range up to the Mercedes S500 which costs more than $90,000.

Trends: As auto buyers increasingly have resisted high prices, luxury car makers have dropped prices on a few individual models, such as the Mercedes C220, to about $30,000.

Luxurious sport utilities such as the Land Rover models and the Toyota Land Cruiser have attracted some buyers away from luxury cars.

Pluses: Good looks, great ride, and respect from your friends and the valet parking attendant.

Minuses: If you do not care a lot about the cachet, you are probably paying too much for the brand name when you could get good looks and comfort for thousands less.

Sporty Cars

Description: These coupes and convertibles put a premium on dashing looks, speedy performance, and good handling. No need to worry about roominess here. These cars are all about panache.

Models: This catch-all category includes flat-out sports cars such as the Chevrolet Corvette and the Porsche models as well as teen-dream power coupes and convertibles like the Ford Mustang and Chevrolet Camaro. Even some sporty versions of luxury models fall in here. Others usually counted in this category are Audi Cabriolet, BMW Z3, Buick Riviera, Cadillac Eldorado, Dodge Viper, Eagle Talon, Ford Probe, Honda Prelude, Lexus SC400, Mercedes S series convertibles, Lincoln Mark VIII, Mazda Miata, Mitsubishi Eclipse, Toyota Celica, and Volkswagen Cabriolet.

Price: The range for these cars fans between about $18,000 for the Chevy Camaro to a superluxe $90,000 for the Mercedes SL500 convertible.

Trends: Once the cutting edge for car enthusiasts, sporty car sales have dwindled in recent years. Some of that excitement has shifted to hot-selling sport utilities. But a racy new model like the BMW Z3, featured in the James Bond movie *Goldeneye*, can still generate car show oohs and ahs.

Pluses: If your pulse quickens looking at or test-driving one of these cars, you understand their allure.

Minuses: If you have a family, you won't have enough space for the kids and their gear. Even for a romantic vacation for two, you might run a little short of luggage space.

Minivans

Description: Originally a smaller version of business vans, these comfortable all-purpose haulers bear little resemblance now to the spartan vans plumbers or electricians might drive. Minivans can seat up to eight people with two rear seats installed. And those rear seats also come out for maximum hauling capacity of everything from plywood to a baby's playpen.

Models: Passenger vans include Chevrolet Astro, Chrysler Town & Country, Dodge Caravan, Ford Windstar, GMC Safari, Mazda MPV, Mercury Villager, Nissan Quest, Plymouth Voyager, and Toyota Previa.

Price: Costs vary from around $17,000 for the base-model Dodge Caravan to $32,000 for the most luxurious Toyota Previa.

Trends: Since Chrysler Corp. (Chrysler, Dodge, and Plymouth models) pioneered this category, minivans have grown to be America's family vehicle, displacing station wagons (although a few wagons still are made). The 1996 redesign of the Chrysler vans seems to have reenergized sales after a leveling off.

Pluses: You really *can* fit it all in. And, the front seat passenger can walk to the rear seats to check kids or cargo without stopping the vehicle.

Minuses: The all-American family image may seem to some of your friends like a dowdy, no-style look. You are not likely to get as many compliments as if you bring home a sport utility.

Sport Utilities

Description: Descended from the big four-wheel-drive Jeeps, Broncos, and Blazers beloved by hunters and fishermen, today's smaller versions are more often driven to the mall than off-road to a trout stream. You also get a lot of capacity for people and gear, but not as much as with a van. Rear seats fold down but do not come out.

Models: "Sport utes," as they are called in Detroit, include Chevrolet Blazer, Chevrolet Suburban, Chevrolet Tahoe, Ford Bronco, Ford Explorer, Ford Expedition, Geo Tracker, GMC Jimmy, GMC Suburban, GMC Yukon, Jeep Cherokee, Jeep Grand Cherokee, Land Rover Discovery, Land Rover Range Rover, Mitsubishi Montero, Oldsmobile Bravada, Suzuki Sidekick, Toyota 4-Runner, and Toyota Land Cruiser. A recent addition to the luxury utility ranks is the Lexus LX 450.

Price: In another wide range, the prices run from about $13,000 for the base-model Suzuki Sidekick to $55,00 for the Range Rover.

Trends: As one of the hottest categories of U.S. vehicles, utilities have doubled in sales in the last five years to nearly 10% of all cars and light trucks now sold. Everybody can find something in this category, from the small Suzuki Sidekicks and Geo Trackers for first-time buyers to the huge Chevrolet Suburbans beloved by people who pull horses in trailers (and those who want to look as if they did).

Pluses: You get cachet and hauling capacity in the same vehicle, and four-wheel drive can be reassuring in snowy or rainy weather.

Minuses: Bigger engines than most vans cut gas mileage to about 15 MPG in the city and the low 20s on the highway. Hot sales have pushed up prices and make it harder to get a good deal here than in most other categories.

Pickups

Description: In the past pickups featured one bench seat in front and an open bed in back. Now they are available with bucket seats, sophisticated sound systems, and other creature comforts. Many pickup owners buy caps to cover the bed.

Models: With their numbered series and myriad variations, pickup models can seem confusing. But the basic lines include Chevrolet C series and K series and the Chevy S-10, Dodge Dakota and Dodge Ram, Ford F150 and Ford Ranger, GMC Sierra and GMC Sonoma, Mazda B series, and Toyota T-100 and Toyota Tacoma.

Price: Base models of the smallest pickups still start below $12,000, with the best-equipped models of full-size pickups hitting $20,000.

Trends: When Bob Seger sings "Like a Rock," the Chevrolet truck ads show cowboys and construction crews at work. But about half the pickups today are sold for "personal use." Pickups can go to the mall as well as to the grain elevator.

Pluses: Lower prices make pickups seem very affordable versus most other categories. And you get lots of hauling capacity. New optional extra-large cabs let you haul up to five people.

Minuses: What you are hauling may get wet when it rains unless you have a cap. Safety equipment such as dual air bags still is not standard in all pickups.

Don't Be Pigeonholed

Starting with the auto companies and their elaborate market research, everyone has an idea about who wants certain vehicles and why. But if you are willing to think beyond the categories and images projected in the television ads and look at what features you like and dislike about various categories and individual vehicles, you may be able to make an unconventional choice that gives you exactly what you need. And in some cases the switch may save you thousands of dollars. For instance, if you need four-wheel drive because of snowy winter roads, but your environmental conscience (or your pocketbook) isn't comfortable with sport utilities, consider the **Subaru Legacy Outback.** You will get all-wheel drive (which automatically adjusts to road conditions) and some of the rugged exterior looks of a utility. In addition, the Subaru's list price is about $4,000 less than a next-to-top-of-the-line Ford Explorer XLT. The Legacy's EPA-rated gas mileage is 22 MPG in the city and 29 on the highway—compared with 15 MPG city, 20 highway, for the Explorer. What you won't get is the high, king- or queen-of-the road driving position or the hauling capacity of a sport utility. But you may still have just what you need. Four-wheel-drive Subaru wagons long have been a favorite in states like Maine and Vermont, where heavy snows are a fact of life. If you often haul more than five people but you like the looks of sport utilities, the **Mazda MPV** gives you seating for seven with squared-off utility looks.

If a moderate amount of hauling capacity and saving money is your concern more than image or bad-weather capability, consider the old-fashioned two-wheel-drive station wagon. Mostly supplanted by vans and sport utility vehicles (SUVs), a few good ones still are for sale. The **Buick Century Special** wagon recently still listed for under $20,000, as did Japanese brands **Toyota Corolla** and **Honda Accord** wagons. The smaller **Saturn SW1 and SW2** wagons had list prices under $15,000.

If all notions of vans, SUVs, and station wagons are at odds with your self-image, but you still need a lot of room, think about breaking the mold entirely and check out a used **Cadillac** or **Lincoln Town Car.** You likely can get a two-year-old model in the mid-20s (see Chapter 14 for more on buying a used car). You will be cruising in elegance, looking more like a sport than a sportsman, but still with 20–25 cubic feet of cargo space, a range similar to those of large- to medium-size station wagons such as the Buick Century.

CHAPTER 2

Your Auto-Biography: The Right Car or Truck for the Job

Now that you've identified a broad target for the price range and size of the vehicle you want, it's time to get more specific. To prepare an accurate auto-biography, you must consider three crucial questions:

- How many people do I need to carry?
- How much luggage or gear?
- What is the primary purpose of this car?

Let's explore each in turn.

Passengers

1. What is the largest number of people you are likely to haul in your vehicle at least every few months?

Two_____ Three to Four_____ Five but not More_____ Six to Eight_____

DIAGNOSIS: if you answered "Two" to the above question, consider anything you want, even a two-seater sports car.

If you answered "Three to Four" to Question 1, you can consider almost anything, starting with a four-door sedan and moving to larger choices.

If "Five but Not More" is your magic number, a large sedan, station wagon, or sport utility will fill the need. If those five people come with gear, go for the wagon or the SUV.

If you said "Six to Eight," you need a minivan. (Your limit for comfortable seating is seven if the van has bucket seats in the second row.)

If you are a Little League coach who drives the starting nine plus their gloves and bats, consider a full-size van such as a Ford Club Wagon or a Dodge Ram Wagon.

Luggage and Gear

1. What is the largest item or combination of items you are likely to carry in your vehicle every few months?_____

2. What (in inches) is the length_____, width_____, and height_____ of that regular cargo?

Do some measuring before you answer the second question. (Seriously.) If you need to, stack together a typical trip's luggage or gear. Or measure around the baby's playpen or whatever your largest cargo is.

When you have filled in these numbers, divide each one by 12 to convert it to feet. Multiply the three numbers together to get a rough estimate of the cubic feet of cargo space that you need.

DIAGNOSIS: If your number is under 15 cubic feet, you will be fine with a compact sedan such as a Saturn, Toyota Corolla, or Buick Skylark.

If your total comes in between 15 and 20 cubic feet, you probably need a sedan such as a midsize Ford Taurus or Mercury Sable (16 cubic feet) or large Oldsmobile Eighty-Eight (18). A step up in space are the Ford Crown Victoria and Mercury Grand Marquis, with 21 cubic feet of cargo space each.

If your number falls in the range of 30–40 cubic feet, a mid-size wagon like the Ford Taurus (38 cubic feet) will carry your goods with the backseat folded down.

When you need to haul more than 40 cubic feet of stuff, you have moved into the sport utility (around 40 cubic feet with the backseats open, 70–80 cubic feet with the seats folded) or van territory. A three-seat minivan can haul about 50 cubic feet with all the seats in but can pile in nearly 150 cubic feet with the rear seats removed.

But within those categories, hauling ability can vary considerably. Therefore it helps to visualize real items in your future van or sports utility. For instance, in a recent review *Car and Driver* magazine usefully determined that the Ford Explorer XLT could haul 35 cases of beer with the seats folded, while arch-competitor Jeep Grand Cherokee Limited could fit in just 28 cases. For non–party animals, the Explorer could carry a 77-by-48-inch sheet of plywood, compared with a 61-by-38-inch sheet in the Grand Cherokee.

Sometimes hauling requirements are very specialized. A colleague of mine is married to a professional cellist who drives to concerts regularly. The family now has leased a series of Toyota Corolla station wagons because competitors in the same price and size range will not accommodate the wife's cello.

When you are still considering various models, you can get the cargo capacity numbers from brochures that dealers give you or from books available at newsstands, such as *Edmund's New Car Prices* ($14.99 recently with CD-ROM). Better yet, you can get the data free on the Internet from the electronic newsstand, where Edmund's and other services post data (http://www.edmunds.com). And most manufacturers post such specifications on their own home pages as well. (See Chapter 6 for more details on getting auto data on the Internet and commercial on-line services.)

Eventually, however, you will want to see the cars or trucks in living, driving color at an auto show or dealer's showroom. (Chapter 6 also discusses the best technique for seeing and test-driving vehicles.) That also gives you a good chance to measure cargo spaces. But if your needs are as specialized as that professional cellist I know, don't just measure the cargo area. Take your equivalent of her cello (golf clubs, maybe) along to a dealer's lot and make sure it will fit before you ever start negotiations about that car, truck, or van.

Purpose

If you are buying a new or used car, what is the major reason you need it? Commuting? Running errands? Hauling kids? Weekends? Vacations? Of course, you will use your vehicle for several things, but one purpose is likely to predominate. Here is a rundown of the major reasons people buy cars and trucks, with some suggestions of best-buy vehicles in each category.

COMMUTING: SHORT HAUL

If you are one of life's geographically lucky who live only a few miles from where you work—or if you commute by train or bus and drive to the station—you may be looking for short-haul transportation. If another family member is driving the principal family vehicle, you probably want to spend as little as you can for your daily ride. Therefore, buying a used car is probably attractive here, especially if you can get a manufacturer's or dealer's warranty or other indication the car or truck is reliable enough to get you to work or the station every day. (For detailed advice on buying used cars, see Chapter 14.)

Since gas mileage is not much of an economic issue when you are driving fewer than 15 miles a day, low-mileage pickups or sport utilities can be as suitable for the short commute as cars. But beware. These trucks frequently are more popular targets for thieves than are cars. You may want to think twice before letting them sit in company or railroad station parking lots, where security may be minimal. (For a list of vehicles most and least likely to be stolen, see Chapter 3.)

Best Buys: If you are considering an inexpensive new car for this category (unfortunately this has come to mean $12,000 or less), three of the most reliable and user-friendly are the least expensive models of the **Geo Metro, Honda Civic, and Toyota Tercel.** While not crucial for short commutes, these entries nonetheless have the added advantage of gas mileage of 30 MPG or more in city driving as rated by the Environmental Protection Agency.

COMMUTING: LONG HAUL

If you are among those Americans who drive for a half hour or more to and from work, your commuting needs change. Riding comfortably in highway driving is likelier with a larger, heavier car if you can afford it. If you tune in your favorite disk jockey or pop in CDs during your morning and evening drives, the quality and ease of operation of the sound system may matter a lot to you. And with a long commute, low gas mileage starts to add up the monthly costs. With highway mileage mostly below 20 MPG, sport utilities are not ideal commuters. Even so, a survey of recent new-vehicle customers shows that for 77% of sport utility buyers and 62% of minivan owners, driving to work is at least one intended use. But 64% of utility buyers and 76% of van drivers intend to take vacation trips in the vehicle, compared with 51% for all car and truck buyers. So a van or sport utility starts making more sense if you use it not only for commuting, but for family fun as well.

Best Buys: **Chevy Lumina, Nissan Altima, Toyota Camry.** You still can get the less luxurious models of these three sedans for under $18,000. All three provide a comfortable ride, easy-to-manage controls from the driver's seat, and gas mileage rated at about 20 MPG in city driving and close to 30 MPG on the highway.

DOING BUSINESS

If your job involves hauling construction supplies or making sales calls in your car, you already have plenty of experience with what kind of car or truck you need. But if you just drive clients to lunch or meetings occasionally, don't forget that shoe-horning a six-footer or a woman in a short-skirted suit into the undersized backseat of a coupe is not likely to improve client relations. If such driving is part of your routine, look for roomy backseats and easy access. (For financial angles on a car used for business, see the end of Chapter 4.)

Best Buys: Four-door versions of the three long-haul commuting picks mentioned previously will fill the bill. Among larger cars selling in the mid-$20,000 range, other good, roomy choices include the **Mazda Millenia, Nissan Maxima GLE,** and the **Volvo 850 GLT.** Look for manufacturer-sponsored bargain lease deals on these cars—especially if you can deduct part of the lease payments as related to business use.

TRANSPORTING THE FAMILY

Being able to fit in all the kids and all their stuff has made minivan sales zoom. Sales of these carry-alls on wheels rose from 1% of all trucks (manufacturers count all vans and sport utilities as well as pickups in their truck division sales) in 1983 to 19% of all trucks—and 8% of all *vehicles*—in 1995. They ride and park like cars. They are easy to get into. Their gas mileage—with highway numbers often in the mid-20s—is good enough to make commuting or vacation trips economical. And the cheapest models still start below $18,000.

Despite some beefing about minivans' "mommy mobile" image, somebody out there must love them. Auto industry research shows that seven out of 10 minivan owners buy another one. Chrysler's redesign of its vans for 1996—introducing sliding doors on both sides of the van—seems to have sparked new enthusiasm among would-be vanners.

If you like the roominess, comfort, and conveniences like the front seat passenger's ability to move to the backseat to check kids or gear without stopping the vehicle, a van is probably for you.

Best Buys: Chrysler brought the first minivan to market, and its **Dodge Caravan, Plymouth Voyager,** and more luxurious **Chrysler Town & Country** still are the leaders. The **Ford Windstar,** with a good safety record, roomy dimensions, and easy-to-remove seats, is nonetheless a relatively slow seller. Look for rebates and other deals.

SPORTING AND SCHLEPPING

Matt Idema, a 24-year-old Chicago consultant shopping for a Jeep Cherokee or an Isuzu Rodeo, is the very image many people hold of a sport utility buyer. "I do a lot of fly-fishing in Michigan, and I don't want to take a car on rough trails," he told *USA Today*. But if many sport utility owners would like to think of themselves like Idema, most act more like van owners. An estimated 70% of four-wheel-drive utility vehicles are never driven off paved roads, surveys show. Nonetheless sport utilities—including the under-$15,000 smaller vehicles like Suzuki Sidekick and Geo Tracker favored by students and other young drivers—seem to have captured what excitement Americans still feel about their cars, an enthusiasm once directed at two-seat sports cars or other speedy and sporty models.

Another part of the attraction reflected in growing sport utility sales is a feeling that the four-wheel-drive option can cope with any weather conditions. "A sport utility owner feels that if a heavy snow falls during working hours, he or she will still be able to get home," explains Dave Kalmus, a vice president at Glendale, California, auto research firm the Dohring Company.

Women make up more than one-third of the buyers of new sport utilities, and a Dohring survey found an astonishing 31% of women ages 35–49 intending to buy a sport utility as their next vehicle. Research shows that women traditionally have cared more about vehicle safety than men when buying cars. So the growing clout of women buyers in SUVs has helped push developments such as installation of both driver and passenger air bags in most of the full-size utilities even before they were required by government regulation.

Best Buys: **Ford Explorer** is the clear-cut sales leader, perhaps partly because its models are priced at least $1,000 less than comparable Jeep Grand Cherokees. But the Jeeps, long dominating this category, still are rated best if you really are an off-roader. **Nissan Pathfinder,** newly redesigned for 1996, has the smoothest, most carlike ride. If you need to haul more but still want a sport utility, try a bigger **GMC Yukon.** But its strong popularity probably precludes a great deal.

KEEP ON TRUCKIN'

Some people—more and more in recent years—just like trucks. Full-size and compact pickups together have been selling 3.7 million vehicles a year—only slightly less than the 4 million for all midsize cars. Pickups can do some hauling jobs—like carrying new trees to put into your yard or your neighbor's—that even vans cannot match.

More important for many people, reasonably comfortable ride and other creature comforts are available in pickups along with that hauling capacity at lower prices than for cars. A handful of small pickups still have a list price below $11,000. Even many full-size pickups carry MSRPs in the $15,000 range.

Best Buys: You probably can buy a **Mitsubishi B2300** for close to $10,000, and its better than average mileage (22 MPG city/27 MPG highway) is helpful if you want to drive your truck to work. Full-size truck lovers might consider the recently redesigned **Ford F-150,** the best-selling single vehicle in the United States. The F-150s start around $15,000 list price and range up above $17,000. If you need seating for up to five, the **Toyota Tacoma Xtracab** has an MSRP of around $18,000.

SHOWING OFF

You've made it, and you want everyone to know it while getting a soft ride, great sound, and pinpoint climate control. Mercedes, BMW, and Lexus are the blue-chip names here. But if you want luxury and comfort without paying for that import image, the Lincoln Town Car remains a strong performer and the once maligned Cadillac division of General Motors has perked up its design and handling and come through with innovations like the high-tech Northstar engine.

Best Buys: For this stratospheric price level, the **Mercedes E-320** is reasonable. Priced in the mid-40s, it made a big hit with owners who got in on its 1995 debut. Listed at a few thousand less, the **Infiniti J30** often is available with discounted price or leasing deals. Buyers who prefer domestic vehicles may find the **Buick Park Avenue,** priced in the mid-30's, a good value.

In thinking over what vehicle you need, be careful not to limit your response to today's situation. Think ahead as long as you are likely to keep the car—maybe five years or more, if that is the case. "People may buy a four- or five-seat vehicle now when their children are two and four years old," cautions AutoAdvisor's Ashly Knapp. "But they forget that in a couple of years the older child will want to bring along a friend, and after that the younger one will, too. Suddenly they cannot fit everybody in."

CHAPTER 3

Staying Safe, Saving Money

Some doting parents are fond of saying that keeping their family safe is precious beyond price. But when it comes to cars and trucks, keeping safe also can save money. That is because the vehicles that are the most crash-worthy and felon-proof also cost the least to insure. While no one wants to choose a vehicle solely for its safety record or a lower than average chance of catching the eye of thieves, those issues make great tiebreakers once you have narrowed down your picks to a handful of sedans, vans, pickups, or sport utilities.

Right Car, Lower Bills

Choosing a model with a better than average safety record can save $200 a year or so from insurance bills that can readily run more than $1,000 per vehicle in the more expensive urban areas even for

STAYING SAFE, SAVING MONEY

drivers with no record of accidents. Discounts for air bags can cut another 5%–15% off the bill, depending on the location and the insurance company. The savings can be even greater for choosing a model not popular with thieves: in the most extreme comparisons a thieves' favorite sport utility model, the Mitsubishi Montero, can cost nearly $900 more to insure than a competitor more likely to be ignored on the street (see details following). And the most effective antitheft devices, such as automatic engine cutoff switches, can cut another 15%–20% from your insurance bill.

In the past, while battling government safety regulations, Detroit's Big Three (Chrysler, Ford, General Motors) argued that the public did not care much about a car's safety record. But lately that argument has gone the way of tail fins. Now those same manufacturers eagerly advertise air bags and other safety devices in their latest models because they have realized how much their customers do care. "Safety is at the top of auto buyers' wish list," says Wall Street analyst Philip Fricke, who follows the auto industry for Prudential Securities.

The numbers back him up. A survey by the Insurance Institute for Highway Safety—a research organization funded by insurance companies—found that 67% of would-be car buyers believed the availability of air bags in a vehicle is very important. First minivans, then sport utilities, started installing driver- and passenger-side air bags three years or more before required by the federal government in order to get a jump on their competitors. When Ford's redesigned Explorer was the only 1995 model among the high-volume sport utilities to offer dual air bags, its sales surged 42% over the previous calendar year to 395,000. Dual air bags now are available at least as options in most cars and minivans. But laggards remain among sport utilities and pickup trucks. Check whether you can get both-side air bags early in your search for the right model—possibly allowing you to eliminate some choices right away.

The air bags now available in most vehicles protect against so-called frontal crashes, where a car or truck crashes head on

31

into another vehicle or fixed object such as a tree or light pole. The National Highway Traffic Safety Administration (NHTSA) estimates that air bags prevent fatal injuries in 29% of such crashes. But side-impact or T-bone crashes—where one car slams into the side of another—kill an estimated 9,000 people a year in the United States. Traditional air bags do nothing to protect against such crashes. Beginning with the 1997 model year, all passenger cars must meet a new federal standard for stronger construction to withstand such side-impact crashes better. But even more promising is the beginning of a trend toward side-impact air bags. Because such innovations are costly, they typically begin with luxury cars. The Volvo 850 installed side-impact bags with its 1995 models, and Mercedes and BMW also have put them in some models.

Recent research has raised some concern that the explosive opening of air bags can pose a danger to small children. Federal safety officials estimate that perhaps 20 children have been killed by air bags. Federal safety officials are considering whether to start requiring an on-off switch for air bags that parents could use when a child is riding in front. For now, this danger can be avoided by having children under 12 ride in the backseat, where there are no air bags. Even more important is to install the safety seats for infants in what is their proper location—the rear seat. For slightly larger children of one year old or more, some models offer built-in child safety seats in the backseat. Introduced by Chysler's minivans, such seats now also are available on some Ford and General Motors minivans.

Choosing a Safe Car

To find a car, truck, van, or sport utility that will keep your family safe, give you peace of mind, and save some money on insurance costs, follow these principles in narrowing down your list of potential choices.

BIGGER IS SAFER

Within the limits of your budget, get the largest vehicle that you can. The laws of physics dominate what happens in a traffic accident: when a larger vehicle collides with a smaller one, the occupants of the larger one almost always fare better. In statistics kept by the Highway Loss Data Institute, another research arm of the insurance industry, 19 of 24 cars that fall into the worst category for injuries occurring in accidents are small cars. "In relation to their numbers on the road, small vehicles account for more than twice as many occupant deaths as large ones," warns the institute.

CHECK THE CRASH TESTS

While bigger is safer, variations still can be wide in the safety of two cars or trucks within the same category. Each year the National Highway Traffic Safety Administration smashes 30–35 of the most widely driven new and redesigned cars into a fixed barrier at 35 MPH—approximating the force of two identical cars hitting head on at that speed. The agency then determines all probable leg, head, and chest injuries the driver and passengers would have suffered, assuming all safety equipment worked as intended. Although manufacturers make cosmetic changes in models almost every year, the crash test results are valid for the three to five years that typically elapse before a given model gets a bumper-to-bumper redesign. Here is a selection of cars, trucks, and vans that fared best in each category in these crash tests. In the one (worst) to five (best) star system that the NHTSA now uses to score these crash tests, the vast majority of vehicles attain an acceptable three stars each for driver and passenger impact. In our list below, best vehicles here scored at least four stars each for driver and passenger. Our rankings include only midsize sport utilities and compact pickups. Large pickups and utilities almost all fared well in crash tests. (For a full list of models, including all utilities and pickups, please see the appendix.) To get the latest results each year, you can call NHTSA at 1-800-424-9393.

BEST IN THE CRASH TEST

In this list of best performers, where two names are listed together (such as Chrysler Sebring/Dodge Avenger), they are "corporate twins." That is, the same car is marketed under two different names by the company.

Subcompacts
Ford Aspire
Geo Metro
Honda Civic
Nissan Sentra
Saturn SL

Compacts
Chrysler Sebring/Dodge Avenger
Ford Probe
Mazda 626DX
Toyota Camry

Midsize
Audi A6
Chevrolet Camaro/Pontiac Firebird
Ford Mustang
Ford Thunderbird

Large
Chrysler New Yorker
Ford Crown Victoria
Infiniti J30

Minivans
Ford Windstar
Honda Odyssey
Pontiac Trans Sport

Sport Utilities (midsize)
Ford Explorer
Jeep Cherokee
Mitsubishi Montero

Pickups (compact)
Dodge Dakota
Ford Ranger

EYEBALL THE REAL-WORLD DATA

The NHTSA crash tests just cited show how well different vehicles hold up in a certain kind of crash under test-track conditions. In terms of a car's likely safety, this is a valuable piece of information. But another source of data reflects real-world experience with injuries where insurance claims are paid that were sustained in traffic accidents involving cars, vans, sport utilities, and pickup trucks. The Highway Loss Data Institute collects these statistics. Though they typically are based on models two years earlier than those currently on sale, like the crash tests, the results remain valid until a vehicle is redesigned totally. Unlike the crash tests, where the vast majority of vehicles nowadays score at least an acceptable three out of five possible stars, the insurance data show a broad range of frequency of injury claims from the best to worst car or truck in a given category. Frequently the worst performer has an injury claim rate more than twice that of the best. Therefore our listing in various categories will show the best and worst finishers. (While the institute separates two- and four-door cars, we are com-

bining those two body styles into large, medium, and small cars for this listing.)

Since these are real-world data, they reflect some real-world biases such as who drives the car. A category might register higher claims partly because it has a high percentage of younger, less experienced drivers. But there are some surprises as well. Sporty cars, while having a predictably high incidence of collision claims (and resulting high insurance costs), rank mostly better than the average for all vehicles for injury claims. Other small cars—two- and four-door—as expected, have a high rate of injury claims, with 19 of 27 small car listings in the highest category of 30% or more worse than average.

Here are the best and worst ratings (for a listing of 170 models, see the appendix):

SMALL CARS

BEST	WORST
Eagle Talon 4WD	Hyundai Scoupe
Saturn SC	Hyundai Excel
Ford Escort	Toyota Paseo

MIDSIZE CARS

BEST	WORST
Oldsmobile Cutlass Supreme	Hyundai Sonata
Volvo 850	Honda Civic coupe
Buick Regal	Pontiac Sunbird
Pontiac Grand Prix	Nissan Altima

LARGE CARS

BEST	WORST
Chrysler Concorde	Mercury Cougar
Buick LeSabre	Ford Thunderbird
Oldsmobile 98	Eagle Vision
Buick Park Avenue	Dodge Intrepid

LUXURY CARS

BEST

Mercedes S Class (long)
Cadillac DeVille
Chrysler LHS
Lexus LS 400

WORST[*]

BMW 3 series
Lexus GS 300
Infiniti J30
————

*While at the bottom of luxury entries, all these cars are still better than the average vehicles for injury frequency.

MINIVANS

BEST

Chrysler Town & Country
Dodge Caravan 4WD
Mercury Villager
Toyota Previa 4WD

WORST[*]

Mazda MPV
Ford Aerostar
Toyota Previa 2WD
Chevrolet Astro

*These vans are better than the average for all vehicles except for the Mazda MPV, which is 28% worse than average.

SPORT UTILITIES*

BEST

GMC Yukon
Toyota Land Cruiser
Ford Explorer 4WD
Jeep Grand Cherokee 4WD

WORST

Nissan Pathfinder[†]
Isuzu Rodeo 2WD
Isuzu Rodeo 4WD
Toyota 4-Runner[†]

*This is true for midsize utilities only. Large Chevrolet and GMC Suburbans have even better injury rates. Small utilities such as Geo Tracker and Isuzu Amigo have worse rates.
†Vehicle redesigned since this data collected.

PICKUPS*

BEST   WORST

BEST	WORST
Chevrolet T-100 series 4WD	Isuzu
Ford Ranger series 4WD	Mitsubishi
GMC T-15 series 4WD	Toyota
Mazda 4WD	Nissan

*This is true for compact pickups only. All rated large pickups are at least 20% better than the average vehicle for injury frequency.

While data on injuries sustained in different cars, trucks, vans, and sport utilities can help you select a likely candidate, your own experience will be affected by its safety devices and other features. When you start inspecting a vehicle at a showroom or auto show, check for these crucial factors:

- Does the car or truck come with an automatic braking system—often abbreviated as ABS? While there is some controversy among insurance companies about how much such brakes have decreased the frequency of accidents, they are likely to help, especially if you often drive on slick, icy, or rainy roads.
- From the driver's seat, do you have an unobstructed view in all directions? If roof pillars or other features make it hard to see in certain spots, this can be dangerous.
- Can you reach all pedals and controls with the seat adjusted well back from the steering wheel? While air bags are chiefly a danger to improperly seated small children, the driver still wants to sit back from the air bag that would burst out from the steering wheel in a collision.
- Do the seat belts seem easy to move across your body, lock, and release? If they do not, you might develop the dangerous habit of rarely using them.

Thinking about Theft

No one wants to take time out from visions of whizzing down the highway or up the trail in your new car or truck to consider how likely that new vehicle is to be stolen. But that is just what you need to do. Owning a vehicle favored by auto thieves can boost your insurance bills as much as or more than buying a model with high collision losses. We will tell you below what models are the most and least likely to vanish from the parking lot while you are shopping in the mall. But keep in mind that whatever model you buy, your danger of losing a car to theft is much greater than it used to be. Car owners and insurance companies lose an estimated $7.5 billion a year to auto theft.

Today's typical auto thief is not a teenage joyrider, but a pro with links to a well-organized larceny ring. Often, in fact, he has been hired to steal a specific model to fill a customer's order. Cars that fall into such hands rarely end up abandoned by the side of the road. Instead they are shipped to buyers overseas or else dismantled and the parts sold separately. Consider these insurance industry statistics: If your car was stolen in 1970, you had approximately a 60% chance of recovering it in sufficiently good condition to be driven again. Today you have a 30% chance.

Even having an aging car does not protect you from auto theft. Operators of so-called chop shops typically make two to four times the value of an intact used car by cutting it up and selling the parts separately. According to data compiled by the National Insurance Crime Bureau—yet another insurance industry research group—in a given year thieves steal more seven-year-old cars than almost-new cars from the current model year.

39

High Theft, High Costs

Whether you are looking at a new or used car, you need to be aware of what its theft record can do to the so-called comprehensive section of your auto insurance—which covers vandalism, fire, and flooding as well as theft. To see the difference that theft statistics can make in your insurance bills, particularly if you live in a high-theft urban area, compare the rates on top theft target Mitsubishi Montero and the Ford Explorer, a similar sport utility that is less popular with thieves. The Explorer costs $1,400 a year to insure in the New York City area vs. $2,350 for the Montero. In Los Angeles it is $3,120 for the Explorer, $3,995 for the Montero.

Based purely on the number of thefts reported, the car heister's hit parade recently has been topped by the high-volume models Honda Accord, Oldsmobile Cutlass Supreme, Ford Mustang, and Toyota Camry, according to the National Insurance Crime Bureau. But the numbers that you care about even more are those showing how likely any individual vehicle is to be stolen. These numbers from the Highway Loss Data Institute take into account the number of thefts in comparison with how many of any given model are on the road. Here is a rundown of the vehicles most and least likely to be stolen:

MOST LIKELY TO BE STOLEN

Model	Likelihood
Toyota Land Cruiser	23 times average
Mitsubishi Montero 4WD	19 times average
Mercedes S Class long wheelbase	15 times average
Acura Legend two-door	13 times average
BMW 300i series convertible	11 times average
Mercedes SL Class convertible	10 times average

Model	Likelihood
Acura Legend four-door	7 times average
Lexus GS 300	6 times average
Nissan 300ZX	6 times average
BMW 300i series two-door	6 times average

LEAST LIKELY TO BE STOLEN

Model	Likelihood
Chevrolet Lumina four-door	11% of average
Saab 900 four-door	15% of average
Buick Skylark four-door	15% of average
Buick Park Avenue four-door	17% of average
Saturn SW station wagon	19% of average
Buick LeSabre four-door	19% of average
Subaru Impreza four-door 4WD	19% of average
Buick Regal four-door	20% of average
Ford Aerostar minivan 4WD	21% of average
Ford E-150 Club Wagon van	22% of average

Foiling the Thieves

Beyond choosing a vehicle with a low theft rate, you can cut your insurance bill further with antitheft devices. The Club and other add-on devices may at least convince a thief that your car is more trouble to steal than a similar one down the block. But because people frequently leave those steel bars in the backseat instead of installing them on the steering wheel, insurance companies do not give discounts for them. However, automatic electronic kill switches can save you as much as 20% on the comprehensive portion of your insurance. "Passive systems that go on automatically with the locking of the car are the most effective at preventing theft," says senior vice president Kim Hazelbaker of the Highway Loss Data Institute. In fact, insurance regulators in 11 states (Florida, Illinois, Kentucky, Louisiana, Massachusetts, Michigan, New Jersey, New York, Pennsylvania, Rhode Island, and Texas) *require* premium discounts of 10%–20% for such passive antitheft systems.

To see why such kill switches generate discounts, consider the Chevrolet Corvette sports car. Before 1986 the Corvette was 15 times as likely to be stolen as the average vehicle. Then General Motors equipped all new Corvettes with its Pass-Key system, which refuses to turn on the starter motor and fuel pump unless it is activated by a special electronic ignition key. Almost immediately the theft rate for Corvettes dropped from 15 times average to just about 2.5 times average. GM has built similar systems into 71% of its 1996 models. Ford has installed disabling devices in the most expensive versions of its 1996 Mustang and Taurus; and Chrysler is planning to add them on its 1998 models. (Security experts believe Mustang thefts have increased in recent years because the Ford model had no engine-disabling system while GM's competing sports sedans, Chevrolet Camaro and Pontiac Firebird, have had such devices since 1988.) Luxury Japanese and European cars—including Lexus and Infiniti, BMW and Mercedes—also have built-in automatic engine disablers as standard equipment. You can readily find out if a model you are considering does have such an antitheft switch by checking the manufacturer's literature or World Wide Web home page.

Where you live and park your car regularly does, of course, affect how much you worry about car theft. The worst metropolitan area for auto theft, Newark, New Jersey, has a theft rate per 100,000 residents twice as high as city number 25, Portland, Oregon. But you should not assume because you live in a small town or leafy suburb that your car is safe from thieves. "FBI data show thieves increasingly targeting suburbs and smaller towns," cautions the National Insurance Crime Bureau. "There is no such thing as a low-risk area for auto theft."

CHAPTER 4

Your Answers,
Your Deal

Now you know what you want—a midsize sedan, a minivan, a sport utility, or whatever suits your needs. You checked out the safety and theft record. What kind of deal will you look for?

The answer to that question will help determine what you can afford. Will you lease a car or truck or buy it? Will you opt for a new or used version? (Safety and theft projections for most new cars apply to two- or three-year-old used cars as well.) Not so long ago, well-to-do consumers typically considered just one option: buying a new car. But about one-third of new cars now are leased—up from 20% as recently as the early 1990s. Nowadays the stream of well-kept two- and three-year-old cars returning from leases is providing a supply of attractive, reliable used cars that didn't exist before. And innovative used-car superstore chains are making it easier than ever to buy with huge inventories and no-dicker shopping.

The boom in recent years in both leasing and sales of used cars stems from the same source as the growth of leasing: the high price of new cars. The average price paid for a new car—the negotiated final price, not the manufacturer's list price—has risen to about $18,500. With that figure having outraced the growth in median family income, car companies have to be concerned about how many people can afford their cars. So their marketers are always looking for ways to make cars seem more affordable. In addition to offering traditional price rebates on cars that are selling slowly, manufacturers now typically put even more money behind subsidized lease deals that will produce low monthly payments. And those low payments—often 20% or more below the loan payments for buying the same car with the same-length loan—are at least part of the attraction for more than half those who turn to leasing, according to a survey by leading auto research firm J. D. Power & Co.

But beware. Getting low monthly payments is not enough to assure that you will be happy with your deal. Leasing a car is distinctly different from buying and owning it. Leasing may be all wrong for you—or perfect. The trick is to work out what really is affordable for you—and the best deal. Filling in our questionnaire below will help you determine if you are a likely leaser, a natural-born buyer, or somewhere in between.

LEASING TEST

These questions will determine if you are a good candidate for leasing:

1. Do you typically trade for a new car every four years or less? Yes_____ No_____

2. Do you want to avoid a down payment of at least 10% of the car's price that is typical with a loan? Yes_____ No_____

3. Do you hope to be driving a more expensive model than your current car or truck? Yes_____ No_____

4. Do you typically drive fewer than 15,000 miles a year? Yes_____ No_____

5. Do you typically keep your car or truck in good condition, following maintenance schedules and washing it frequently? Yes_____ No_____

6. Do you hate the idea of having to sell or trade your used car when it is time to get a new one? Yes_____ No_____

If you answered "Yes" four or more times, you at least want to consider leasing.

Pluses and Minuses

Leasing is the easiest way to get a new car every few years. Also, it forces the dealer or leasing company (rather than you) to worry about disposing of the old one. In a "closed-end" lease—which describes almost all leases being offered by dealers and manufacturers—the value of your car or truck at the end of the lease will be fixed in advance. Usually you will have an option to buy it at or near that price if you decide to hold on to it rather than lease or buy a new one. Since payments are based not on the total value of the car, but only on its depreciation while you are leasing it, you might, for instance, be able to lease a $43,500 (in 1996) Mercedes E320 for monthly payments similar to those on a loan to buy a $32,820 Buick Park Avenue Ultra. As a result of such math, more than 70% of new-car transactions are leases for some luxury nameplates such as Jaguar.

But leases have some major disadvantages. Potentially one of the biggest—especially if you are not accustomed to leasing—is that you are forced to make a major financial decision when your lease expires. You must either turn that car or truck back and buy or lease a new one or (alternatively) decide to exercise your option to buy the vehicle at the lease-end price known as the "residual value." On the other hand, if you own your car or truck, you can postpone any decision about replacing it at least until mechanical trouble forces your hand.

BUYING TEST

These questions will help you determine if you are a better buyer than leaser:

1. Do you typically keep a car for five years or more? Yes_____ No_____

2. Is the idea of finishing with loan payments and owning your car or truck free and clear important to you? Yes_____ No__

3. Can you readily come up with the down payment of 10% of the purchase price that is the typical for most car loans? Yes_____ No_____

4. Are you casual or even careless about maintenance and keeping your vehicle clean? (Be honest now.) Yes_____ No_____

5. Are you annoyed by the idea that the dealer or leasing company may charge you a penalty if you want to end your lease early or if you return the car or truck in a condition that does not meet their standards? Yes_____ No_____

Three or more "Yes" answers—especially if they include questions 1 and 3—make you a good candidate for buying rather than leasing. Buying a vehicle and driving it until it drops is almost always the least expensive option. In that case, once your loan is paid off, you still have several years of payment-free driving ahead. And if you are among the lucky car or truck owners (22% recently) who are able to pay cash for your vehicle, so much the better. You are avoiding all the interest charges that you would be paying with either a loan or a lease.

Not So Simple

But the question is not always that simple. If you would have to sell stocks or other prospectively profitable investments to raise cash for a new car, you might wind up ahead in the long run if you keep that investment in place and go for a lease with its low up-front cash requirement (typically just a security deposit equal to about one month's payment plus the first month's payment in advance). Some leases require a down payment (known in leasing jargon as a **capital cost reduction**). The best leasing deals, though, avoid any down payment.

SATISFIED LEASERS

There are good and bad reasons for leasing, according to recent research. In a survey of 14,000 people who were leasing vehicles, Detroit-based Strategic Research & Consulting Group found that the 23% of those responding who had shopped almost exclusively for the lowest possible monthly payment were the least satisfied with leasing and the least likely to lease again. Those who were happiest with their leases "recognize that leasing gives them the opportunity to get more car for the money with less hassle and more peace of mind." If you think you fit into that group (18% of the total surveyed), then leasing probably will make you, as this group is labeled, a "smart shopper."

If you look like a leaser, check out Chapter 10 for more details on assessing whether a specific lease deal is a good one. If you were born a buyer, look at Chapter 7 for advice on finding the best loan deals.

Used but Not Abused

The auto industry's euphemisms for used cars have not improved—they have been calling the cars "pre-owned" since the days of the mercifully disappearing motor-mouthed salesman in the plaid sport coat. But the used-car deals have been getting a lot better. That is especially true if you get one that is in fact not pre-owned, but pre-leased. Because of the requirements mentioned previously that people leasing cars must keep them in good condition or face financial penalties, cars coming off leases typically make the best used cars. As the once torrid American love affair with the car cools off, your friends are not likely to care if you have a new car or almost new. They may admire the deal you got more than the sleek styling. All this has made buying used cars attractive even where it might seem least likely—among those currently leasing new cars. In its survey of people currently leasing, Strategic Research & Consulting found that after a predictable 51% who intended to lease another new car when the current lease expires, the next largest group, 24%, intended to buy a used car. Only 11% planned to buy a new car.

The used cars you can buy today also are more reliable than in the past for reasons beyond the returning lease fleet. In the past 10 years, cars and trucks made in the United States have taken big strides to catch up to the quality and reliability standards previously set by Japanese manufacturers such as Honda and Toyota. With more careful manufacturing and a much greater use of corrosion-resistant materials for body parts, today's two-year-old car or truck that may sell as a used vehicle simply has a longer useful life expectancy ahead of it than its counterpart 10 years ago.

Furthermore, some auto manufacturers—wanting to get in on the booming used-car business and to be sure that their image for reliability is upheld—have begun so-called certification programs for their used cars. These brands—including Infiniti, Jaguar, Lexus, Mercedes-Benz, Nissan, and Saturn—provide warranties of one to three years on their used cars if the car passes a standardized inspection at one of their dealers. Outside such programs, steering clear of used lemons and bad deals is still imperative. (For details on picking and buying a used car, see Chapter 14.) If you choose carefully, for a price on a two-year-old car or truck that can run 60% or less of what you would have paid for that vehicle new, you can be driving reliable and still eye-catching wheels. And since the vehicle is worth less than a new model, your insurance costs will be lower.

Step up to Luxury

Alternatively, buying a one- to three-year-old car may let you step up to a luxury car—where the high incidence of leasing new cars produces a steady stream of returning used models. Even expensive sport utilities can be good used cars now. Once these four-wheel-drive vehicles were a poor risk as used cars because their owners typically had used them to lurch over ruts and rocks on trails in the mountains or the backwoods. But today's average sport utility rarely leaves the highway, and their repair records are no worse than that of cars.

In recent years some manufacturers (starting with Ford) have been leasing used vehicles. Based on the payments alone, this can be attractive. But leasing loses many of its advantages with used vehicles. Much of the reason for leasing is to have a new car with lower payments than if you bought it. And since with a lease you are likely to drive a car only for the first two or three years of its life, you have a good chance of avoiding any major repairs. Leasing a used vehicle, of course, eliminates that advantage.

More Maintenance Ahead

That same drawback is the major negative that comes with buying used cars. If, say, you buy a two-year-old car or truck with 22,000 miles on the odometer, you will be facing maintenance and repair costs sooner than with a new car (see Chapter 5 for more details). These costs and the trouble involved need to be weighed against the money you potentially will be saving by buying used.

But if the economics of buying used seem right for you, the buying experience is likely to be better than in the past. In addition to manufacturer-sponsored warranty and certification programs through traditional dealers, the fast-spreading used-car superstores such as CarMax offer large inventories of all makes of used cars or trucks with no-haggle, one-price selling. And, say many industry analysts, such one-price buying makes more sense with used cars than new because used cars are much harder to compare. "With a new car, there is always a chance of a better bid at another dealer down the road on exactly the same car," says vice president Dave Kalmus of the research firm the Dohring Co. "But each used car is different, with an individual history of mileage and maintenance."

Now that you know whether you want a new car or a used one and whether buying or leasing makes more sense for you, it is time to do some hard-eyed calculation about what you can afford.

Driving for Business: The Finances

If you are buying a car to use entirely or partly for work, especially if you run your own business or are an independent contractor, this may be a factor in both what vehicle you choose and whether you decide to buy or lease. For business use, leasing often produces lower tax bills.

Under 1986 tax law, Congress sharply limited the total business deductions for depreciation of cars that you buy. Adjusted periodically for inflation, that limit recently was about $14,500 total after five years. If you bought a $30,000 car entirely for business use, after five years you could deduct less than half the cost as depreciation.

But if you lease, you can deduct the lease payments, subject to some adjustments. If you use the car partly for personal use, you must prorate the deductions. If that $30,000 car had $400 monthly payments and you used it half the time for business, your monthly deduction would be $200. And the IRS requires you to add back a small amount to your gross income each year to offset the lease deductions (if you get this far, see your accountant for up-to-date IRS tables detailing these figures).

Sizable lease savings.

Lease savings remain big. Using the IRS formula from 1996, a $30,000 car used totally for business with a five-year lease at $400 a month would provide about $20,650 in deductions over that period, compared with the maximum $14,500 in depreciation if you bought the car. The more expensive the car, the bigger the savings. A $40,000 car with $550 monthly payments would generate total deductions of about $27,400 after five years.

Deducts like a truck.

On the other hand, if you prefer to own your vehicle and your business requires you to carry equipment or other supplies, consider a heavy-duty sport utility weighing over 6,000 pounds. That includes all the Land Rovers, the Chevrolet and GMC Suburban, the Chevy Tahoe and GMC Yukon, the Toyota Land

Cruiser, and Ford's recently introduced Expedition. Through a quirk in the 1986 law, intended to cover only trucks owned by businesses, these big utilities qualify for almost total depreciation. A $45,000 Land Cruiser used for business could generate more than $42,000 in depreciation deductions after five years, compared with the $14,500 limit for less weighty vehicles, including all cars. In addition to these sport utilities, some large vans and pickups clear this 6,000-pound hurdle. But check with your accountant before you make a decision based on this provision. The IRS hates loopholes like this one and may convince Congress to close it someday soon.

CHAPTER 5

What Can You Afford? Don't Kid Yourself

That TV pitchman for the big holiday sale or the newspaper ads in the Sunday auto section make new cars sound so affordable—especially with those ultralow lease payments. The people who pay to make those cars sound affordable are car dealers—that's their job. Your job is to see if those deals really are affordable for you. Of course, that means seeing what will fit into your overall budget.

Following the guidelines in Chapters 1 and 2, you have decided what kind of vehicle you need. Here you will see how you can afford to fill that need. In adding up your budget, your biggest potential pitfall is forgetting obscure but mandatory items such as a likely higher cost for insurance on a new car. Starting at the dealer showroom, the suggested retail price you are quoted may not include freight charges—often as much as $500—for shipping the vehicle from the factory to the dealer. Even more costly depending on where you live are state and possibly local sales taxes—which can run as high as 12% but are more typically 5%–8% of the purchase price. And a new (or used) car calls for a new state registration with fees typically running $50–$125. These items usually figure into the total amount you borrow with a loan or finance with a lease—and therefore help determine your real-life monthly payments.

10% to 15% of Monthly Expenses

In setting up your budget, however, you need to go beyond even the cost of buying, taxing, and registering the vehicle. To make a careful decision about what vehicle you can afford to buy, you must also consider other crucial items discussed in this section. In addition, try to think of expenses special to your circumstances. For instance, if you live in a city and are used to parking your old car on the street, you may have to consider paying for a parking lot for the new car because the theft risk is too great. But wherever you live, you must consider these expenses and be sure that you can readily cover them beyond your monthly loan or lease payments and all your other living expenses. "I find most people can comfortably budget 10% to 15% of their monthly living expenses for their car, including insurance and gas," advises Diahann Lassus, a financial planner in New Providence, New Jersey, who often helps clients with budgeting decisions. Following is a rundown of major expenses.

INSURANCE

A new car means higher insurance costs. (Opting for a late-model used car can cut those costs.) Your premiums for liability coverage required of all drivers may not change much from your old car. What will skyrocket is the so-called collison and comprehensive portions of your policy. Collision pays to repair accident damage to your car, while comprehensive covers theft, fire, and natural disasters. You may be in for a shock with your new car, especially if you have been driving a car or truck more than five years old and have dropped collision and comprehensive coverage entirely to save money.

As seen in Chapter 3, you can cut your insurance costs by opting for a vehicle that has a good safety record or relatively low attraction for car thieves. Insurance costs vary not only by model, but by metropolitan areas and even from the city to the suburbs within those areas. So when you have narrowed down the number of cars or trucks on your wish list, call your insurance agent to see what insurance costs would be. While your actual rates will be highly local, we can give you a broad idea of which vehicles cost more or less to insure. The Insurance Services Office compiles such rankings for the insurance industry and supplies them for auto cost rankings annually in **MONEY** magazine. You will find the full list of insurance cost rankings in the appendix. But here is a short list of vehicles that—primarily because of their collision repair costs and theft histories—rank very high or very low in their costs to insure compared with other similar vehicles in the same price range.

An alphabetical list of cars, trucks, vans, and sport utilities:

VERY HIGH INSURANCE COSTS

Geo Metro—two-door hatchback
Ford Mustang—all versions

VERY LOW INSURANCE COSTS
(All Versions of Vehicles Listed)

Buick Park Avenue
Cadillac DeVille
Cadillac Seville
Chrysler Town & Country

Dodge Caravan
Ford Explorer
Ford Taurus
Mercury Sable
Plymouth Voyager

MAINTENANCE

One of the best reasons to buy or lease a new car is to avoid the high repair bills that likely lie just ahead for your old car. But even new cars have maintenance costs, especially after about two years. If all goes well, at first your maintenance bills will be just for oil changes at $50 or less each every 3,000–5,000 miles. But a conscientious owner will think about getting new brakes ($150 or so) at about 20,000 miles and an engine tune-up ($175 or so) at about 30,000 miles. At 40,000 miles it is time for new tires (around $400). Intellichoice, a Compton, California, research firm that specializes in determining the cost of owning various vehicles, calculates that in five years of ownership even low-priced cars will run up maintenance costs of $3,000 or more (including replacement of tires, batteries, and brakes that mostly come in years three, four, and five). For luxury brands—where dealers tend to charge carriage-trade prices for maintenance and repairs—costs will be still higher. And in sport utilities the complications of four-wheel drive can push up bills for maintenance such as wheel alignment.

REPAIRS

Even as the durability of new cars has improved in the last decade, so have the warranties that pick up the cost of any serious repairs. A typical manufacturer's warranty now lasts for three years or 36,000 miles, whichever comes first, instead of the one year/12,000 miles standard in the past. And it typically covers all parts except tires, brakes, and other items cited in the routine maintenance section above. Because of such coverage, Intellichoice figures that repair costs beyond those covered by the warranty typically run in the neighborhood of $500–$1,000 for five years of ownership for most cars, vans, sport utilities, and pickups (with luxury cars like BMW, Jaguar, and Porsche running $1,500–$2,500). If you buy a one- or two-year-old used car, you may be able to pick up the remaining part of the original factory warranty. As we noted, some used cars also now have fresh warranties of their own covering one to three years from their purchase.

DEPRECIATION

Though not an item in your monthly cash budget, depreciation can be a major expense if you are likely to buy a new car and sell it as a used car within four years or if you lease it. To take one comparison, let's look at a Saturn SL1 four-door sedan—recently selling for $11,395—and a Mercury Tracer at $11,755. After three years of ownership the expected trade-in value of the Saturn will be 75% of its original price or $8,500. The Tracer, with just 61% in expected retained value, would be worth $7,176. That $1,375 is a major consideration if you plan to sell or trade after three years. Or, if you were going to lease one of those cars, the monthly payments would be lower for the Saturn because the decrease in value over the three years would be lower. In calculations of total ownership costs, Intellichoice adds in five-year depreciation along with the other costs just cited. "The cheapest car to buy may not be the cheapest car to own," notes Intellichoice president Peter Levy in explaining his firm's approach.

What's Your Old Car Worth?

Depending on the age and condition of what is sitting in your garage now, its value may be an important part of your budget for a new (or newer) car or truck. You eventually must decide whether to trade it in where you buy your new car or sell it yourself (see following). But in calculating what you can afford, it is essential to start out by getting a ballpark idea of what your old vehicle is worth. At this point, keep in mind the rule we mentioned earlier in connection with buying used cars. All new cars of the same make and model are roughly the same, but every used car is different. Your car's specific history—its mileage and condition—will determine its value.

Despite its individuality, start by seeing what your car's family members are worth. Check your library or ask your insurance agent or bank loan officer to show you the *NADA* (National Auto Dealers Association) *Official Used Car Guide* to get some idea of the valuations dealers will be using. Avoid the version of the NADA guide sold at the newsstand because that book gives you only the retail price—not the wholesale or trade-in value.

But at that same newsstand you can pick up *Edmund's Used Cars Prices & Ratings* (recently $6.99), which includes rankings on such items as safety and reliability as well as wholesale and retail prices. The drawback to the Edmund's guide is that it is updated only quarterly. The Edmund's used-car values on the World Wide Web (http://www.edmunds.com) are more timely—and free— if you are handy with a keyboard and a modem. When you use any of these books or Web sites, be sure to check the adjustments for mileage. It can make a big difference. For instance, recently a 1993 Toyota Camry DX sedan was listed in the NADA guide with a trade-in value of $11,025 with less than 50,000 miles on the odometer. With higher mileage that value dropped to $10,600.

Useful as they are, the values in these books typically are national ones, although the NADA guide does have regional editions. You will be selling or trading in a local market, and you will realize it is not only in real estate where location matters. The same three-year-old Jeep Grand Cherokee with its go-in-any-weather four-wheel drive may be worth more as a used car in snowy Denver than in sunny Phoenix. Look at the used-car ads in your local paper or specialized classified ad publication. See how cars like yours seem to be priced.

Finally, get your car detailed so that it is looking its best (this will cost you $100–$150 but will pay off in higher value). Visit the used-car lots of new-car dealers who sell the make of your old car. Ask for bids on your old car and keep careful track of these bids and who made them. You may want to accept one of them later. Even if not, you have a real-world value to place on that car for your budgeting work.

Trade It in or Sell It?

When you have decided to get a new car, it is tempting to avoid the hassle of selling your old car and just to trade it in where you are buying your new one. If you do trade in, however, you cut your chances of getting a good deal overall. As we will discuss in detail in Chapter 12, to get the best price you must know exactly how much you want to pay over dealer cost and negotiate hard toward that goal. When you throw a trade-in into the mix, you complicate the negotiation and tip the advantage toward the car salesman and his manager. They go through such deals several times a day while you tackle the issue only once every few years. Keeping the transactions for your old car and your new one separate from each other leads to the best deal. But if the convenience of trading in means a lot to you, at least do your homework on your old car as previously discussed.

You may be an exception to this rule if you are are driving a wheezing clunker. The extra trouble to sell it is not worth the money involved; take what you can get on the trade-in. Trading in your old car does have one other often overlooked advantage: the sales tax savings. Most states tax only the difference between the new-car cost and the trade-in—not the full purchase price.

For a car or truck in decent condition, though, it makes the most economic sense to place a well-crafted classified advertisement and sell it yourself. But you then have to handle the phone calls of prospective buyers and take the time to show them the car. You may also have legitimate security concerns. You are giving your phone number to strangers and—if they want to see the car—your address as well. One possible solution is to avoid general circulation newspapers. If your company, club, or other organization has a newsletter (or even bulletin board) where you can advertise, use that forum. Calls then will be limited to your fellow employees or members and their friends.

A good middle ground (likely to fetch a price between wholesale and retail) is to sell your vehicle to a used-car operation of a new-car dealer other than one where you plan to buy your new vehicle. That will involve less hassle than selling the car yourself but still will keep your old-car transaction separate.

Leasing, Borrowing, and Budgeting

If you are among the 22% of potential new car owners who are likely to pay cash, your budgeting is pretty simple. You must just make sure that you are not depleting a prudent cash reserve by going this route and that you will be able to handle insurance, maintenance, and repair costs. But if yours will be among the roughly 45% of new-vehicle transactions that involve borrowing or one-third that opt for leasing, determining your potential loan or lease payments is crucial to your budgeting.

If you plan to finance your car, look first at the down payment. While about 10% is the average down payment for new cars involving loans, financial advisers counsel that putting up 20% is preferable if you can do it; a down payment at that level will help assure that you have some equity built up in the car by the time you are likely to trade it for a new one. If you cannot comfortably raise at least 10% of the probable purchase price (see Chapter 6 on how to estimate this price) from the value of your old car or other sources, you probably should consider either leasing this model or buying a less expensive car. Your monthly loan payments will, of course, be determined by how much you need to borrow and the current cost of money—the interest rate you will be charged.

For the same car at the same price, lease payments will be lower than loan payments because you are not financing the total value of the car. Instead the lease amount covers just the difference between what the car is worth new and what it is estimated to be worth after the two, three, or four years that your lease will run. Since most lease deals are advertised by their monthly payments, you can readily get an idea of these with a scan of the local car ads. But check carefully for the fine print in these ads. Make sure the deal does not involve a down payment—often called **capital cost reduction.** Avoiding a down payment is one of the major reasons you are thinking about leasing.

Give careful answers in the worksheet below, and you can start out feeling assured that you are shopping for a car you can really afford. However, avoid the trap of extending the loan for as long as possible to lower the payments. Limit your loan to no more than four years. Not only will a longer loan increase your interest costs, it also will mean that until the late stages of the loan you will not have built up any equity in the car. In extreme cases you could find yourself what the industry calls "upside down"—where the amount due to pay off your loan is greater than your equity. Your trade-in value then amounts to a negative.

YOUR WORKSHEET

1. Maximum monthly car expense you can comfortably pay considering the rest of your budget:_____

2. Monthly cost of insurance:_____
   Plan on setting aside a monthly amount even if the bills come quarterly.

3. Monthly reserve for maintenance:_____
   Leave room to increase this amount after the second year, when maintenance costs will start to rise.

ADD TOGETHER item 2 and item 3 and subtract the total from item 1. Enter the result in item 4.

4. Monthly payment you can afford for a loan or lease:_____
   If you plan to lease, this is the monthly payment you can consider. If you plan to borrow and buy the car, consult the loan table in Appendix D. It will tell you approximately how much loan principal you can finance at various interest rates.

5. Loan amount:_____
   Enter the total you get from the table.

6. Total price you can pay for a car:_____
   If you are planning a 20% down payment, divide the number in line 6 by 0.8. For a 10% down payment, divide by 0.9, and so on. The result will let you see how much you can pay for a vehicle.

7. Combined freight charge and regional advertising fees:_____
You can get the freight charge from price guides or manufacturer's brochure or home page. Regional advertising fees may show up in the fine print of ads, or a dealership can tell you if you call.

8. Subtract item 7 from item 6. Enter result here:_____

9. Take the sales tax rate in your area and add it to 1.0:_____
An 8% rate becomes 1.08, 10% 1.10, and so on.
Divide item 8 by item 9. Enter below.

10. Transaction price you can afford before freight and taxes:_____

Once you have worked your way through this calculation, you will be able to tell whether the car, pickup, van, or sport utility you have been considering is within your means. If your total is way off, grit your teeth and consider a cheaper vehicle. Or, if you have your heart set on your first choice, you may have to make other hard budget choices. "I try to get my clients to decide what really matters to them," says Peg Downey of the financial-planning firm Moneyplan in Silver Spring, Maryland. "For instance, they may have to decide if the expensive new car is more important than the vacation they have been planning."

CHAPTER 6

Getting the Lowdown and Setting Your Price

With cars, as with most financial transactions, good information translates into money in your pocket. In the bad old days not so long ago, car manufacturers and dealers had almost all the information. But increasingly over the last decade, consumers have become better informed by using magazines, price guides, and recently the Internet's World Wide Web. With a little effort you now can find out what a dealer's cost is for a vehicle you might be interested in. You can find out if price rebates, subsidized lease deals, or other special breaks can cut your cost. Best of all, you can decide exactly what you intend to pay for the car or truck before you ever go near a showroom. "By doing careful research, people can achieve their real savings before they ever start negotiating for a car," advises spokesman Jerry Karbon for the Credit Union National Association, an umbrella group for local credit unions.

The first step in deciding what you intend to pay is to avoid thinking about a discount from the car's list price and instead calculate in terms of how much you will have to pay over the dealer's cost. In ads on TV or in newspapers or in the manufacturer's published literature, the price you see is the manufacturer's suggested retail price—the MSRP, or list price. But at any given time only a few vehicles in tremendous demand can in fact sell steadily for that price. (The longest-running modern example is the GMC and Chevrolet Suburban, a big but stylish sport utility. With General Motors keeping production low and cachet high, Suburbans are in such perennial short supply that they rarely sell below list price and occasionally command a premium.) But most other models—including luxury lines—actually sell at 8%–12% below MSRP. Remember those are average prices that take into account all those well-informed, hard-bargaining buyers. The dealer is delighted to sell any given vehicle as close as he can to list price. Don't be the one who gives dealer profits an on-the-spot boost. Thus the first goal of your price research is to find out the dealer's cost.

The Dealer's Cost—Sort Of

The number most often cited as the dealer's cost is the so-called invoice price—the wholesale price that the manufacturer bills the dealer when a new car or truck is shipped to him. But that is not the whole story. An additional amount—descriptively called the **holdback**—is held back by the manufacturer and paid to the dealer later—usually quarterly—in effect cutting the dealer's cost. When a car model is in oversupply, a dealer eager to get it off his lot may negotiate a price that will cut into his holdback—typically around 3% of the MSRP—and thus strike a selling price below the invoice price. In normal circumstances, though, most dealers are unlikely to sell below their invoice price unless there are special incentives. The manufacturer may offer so-called dealer incentives for slow-moving models—in effect rebates paid to the dealer instead of the car buyer. Unlike heavily advertised consumer rebates, these dealer incentives are rarely publicized. But if you have done your homework and know such an incentive exists, you often can negotiate half or more of that amount as savings for yourself.

At the Newsstand

If you still prefer reading your research on the page rather than on the computer screen, you have plenty of alternatives at the newsstand. In March each year—at the start of the spring car-buying season—**MONEY** magazine's new car special report gives you the dealer costs for more than 500 models of cars, vans, pickups, and sport utilities, along with maintenance and other figures needed to compute your total ownership costs. For a focus strictly on price and dealer's costs of not only the basic vehicle, but also of various individual options and options packages, look for *Edmund's New Car Prices* and *Edmund's New Pickup, Van & Sport Utility Prices* ($6.99 each at bookstores and newsstands; $14.99 if accompanied by CD-ROMs showing pictures of vehicles and other details). These books are updated quarterly. To make sure you are aware of any and all rebates or dealer incentives on the vehicles that interest you, it is well worth spending the $7 for an individual issue of a publication called *Car Deals* (800-475-7283). Most rebates last for about three months, although many times they are renewed after that. The *Car Deals* list of price breaks is updated every two weeks, so if your decision about buying a new car takes several months to make, you might want to get a second, up-to-date copy of the newsletter before making your final call. You can save even the small price of *Car Deals* if a library near you stocks the trade paper *Automotive News*. This weekly publication aimed at dealers, executives of auto manufacturers, and others in the industry publishes a continuously updated list of rebates and dealer incentives near the back of each issue.

If you want to get *Car Deals* along with a broader information package, try Fighting Chance (800-288-1134). For $22.95 you will get the latest *Car Deals* plus invoice prices for all trim levels of one vehicle. You can get details on additional vehicles for $5 apiece. A competing service from Intellichoice, the firm that supplies data for **MONEY** magazine, gives you the invoice price rundown on two competing vehicles for $19.95. It is called ArmChair Compare, and the telephone number is 800-227-2665.

Though they are not broken out on the *Car Deals* or *Automotive News* lists, the same models of cars and trucks that carry rebates frequently offer subsidized leases as well. Since leasing is the fastest-growing part of the new-car business, manufacturers now typically put the biggest share of their promotional money behind these leases. Though it takes some work to figure out just how good these deals are (see Chapter 10 for details), spotting them in the first place is pretty easy. Open up the Friday or Sunday special auto section of your newspaper and start scanning for the largest ads talking about leasing. Look for the biggest type and the smallest payments. That may or may not involve a car or truck you want, but you can be pretty sure you have spotted the subsidized lease deals of the moment. (While you are looking at these ads, be sure to read the fine print carefully, as always with lease deals.)

If you feel that you need a jump start to get going with such research, the car loan specialist at your credit union may be able to get you revved up. Many credit unions stock safety information on different models as well as price guides. They may also have a computer hookup that lets you check the latest information on the World Wide Web. A stop at the credit union lets you shop for money (see Chapter 7) and get going on your price research at the same time.

On the Net

The computer hookup at your credit union (or perhaps from a friend's computer) may give the most valuable assistance if you are not among the estimated 30% of new-car buyers who have access on their own at home or in the office to price information on the World Wide Web. Amid all the fevered hype about the information superhighway, new-car prices are one of the few areas where lots of new and useful information has quickly become available on-line. Commercial on-line services all offer dealer-cost information along with new-car reviews. America Online (keyword: AUTOMOBILE) has reviews from *Car and Driver* and *Road & Track*. CompuServe (GO AUTOMOTIVE) picks up reviews from *Automobile* magazine. Prodigy (jump: AUTOMOBILES or CARS) has a service called Autonet that lists new car prices and specifications.

On the Internet's World Wide Web, you may want to check first with the home pages of two or three manufacturers whose cars or trucks interest you. Much of this information is similar to that available in brochures you can get from a dealer, but finding it all on-line can be much easier than traveling to different dealers or waiting for them to mail you the material. These home pages, while self-serving, are a good place to check basic facts such as gas mileage or the cargo capacity of a sport utility or van. For instance, you could check on a Toyota Camry at the Toyota site (http://www.toyota.com).

Probably the most useful site is that maintained by price guide publisher Edmund's (http://www.edmunds.com). The company has put all its new-car and used-car data on the World Wide Web for free (company executives believe that good word of mouth from the Web site sells books to the friends and co-workers of the Web users). And unlike the quarterly updates of its books, the on-line Edmund's data is changed immediately if price increases or other changes are published by the auto companies. Even up-to-date rebate information is at this site for free.

Setting Your Price

You are not, of course, doing all this research about dealer cost just to enrich your knowledge of the auto industry. Your aim is to decide how much over cost you will offer the dealer initially and how much higher than your initial offer you are willing to go. By knowing this in advance, you can keep control of the price discussion. *Start negotiating without such benchmarks, and you are almost guaranteed to pay more than you want to and more than you have to for your new car or truck.* As we will see in Chapter 10, setting a target price is important even if you plan to lease your new vehicle; a leaser who focuses only on payments also is likely to pay too much.

Unfortunately, setting a target price is more complicated than finding out the dealer invoice cost and deciding you are going to bid $200 or $500 or some other number above that. Byzantine though it is, the auto market still responds to supply and demand—especially extremely high demand or extreme oversupply. As we have noted, vehicles where demand steadily runs high, like the Chevrolet Suburban—can command list price and sometimes more. The same is true, although more briefly, for sporty and limited-supply cars such as the BMW Z3, in which the latest James Bond chased babes and bad guys. On the opposite end, Chrysler's full-size sedans Concorde and LHS were selling so poorly recently that dealers were at times striking deals for below invoice price—giving up part of their 3% holdback. Happily, researching for rebates gives you a signal at the same time of cars and trucks where you may be able to strike especially good deals. For instance, Denver attorney Ronald Litvak let a rebate lead him to just such a deal. With the $1,000 consumer rebate, Litvak got a new Chrysler Concorde for 1% below the invoice price after getting bids from two competing dealers in his area.

Deals like Litvak's, however, come along only when a car or truck is in oversupply. On a car or truck selling reasonably well with no special incentives, you get an average deal if you pay 3%–4% over the invoice price for vehicles with list prices under $20,000. On a car with a $15,000 invoice price, therefore, that deal would result in paying $450–$600 over the invoice price. Aim lower—to pay 1%–2% over invoice. On the $15,000-invoice car, start bidding at the invoice price (see Chapter 12) and target a deal at 1%–2% ($150–$300) above invoice.

In general, dealers expect to make a larger profit on luxury cars and other expensive models with list prices over $30,000. If such a model is selling reasonably well, you probably will not be able to strike a deal as close to invoice price as you could with a cheaper model. On a car with a $30,000 invoice price, any deal for less than 5% ($1,500) over that mark is a good price. Margins of 7% or even more are quite common in this price range. Start bidding about 3% ($900) over the invoice price and aim for a deal at 5% over or less. That all changes, though, if a luxury brand is selling poorly. Then look for big-money rebates (often $1,500) to consumers and dealer incentives, which you ought to be able to capture in part as savings for yourself. Slow-selling luxury models are especially likely to offer mouthwatering lease deals.

To start toward setting your target price, get out your price guides or printouts from the World Wide Web and fill in the following worksheet:

YOUR TARGET PRICE

Model Name:_____

Manufacturer's Suggested Retail Price: _____
(Remember to add on any options you want to include. These often must be chosen in groups, with names such as Ford's GT Package, which includes air-conditioning, AM/FM stereo and cassette player, and 10 other items.)

Dealer's Invoice Cost:_____
(Again, remember to include options. Price guides and Web sites will tell you the dealer cost for individual options or packages. In one simple example, a recent version of the Mazda MX-6 sport coupe offered air-conditioning at an MSRP of $900, dealer's invoice of $720.)

Does this model offer a dealer incentive? Yes_____ No_____

If the answer above is "No," make your first offer at the dealer invoice price. If the answer is "Yes," start out at the invoice price minus 70% of that dealer incentive while letting the salesman know you are figuring in the incentive. (With a $1,000 incentive in force, you would bid the invoice price minus $700, for example.)

Your initial bid:_____
(Fill in the result of the computation above.)

You may catch a dealer with a lot full of Tauruses or Accords who can tell you have done your homework and is ready to deal. But if the dealership comes back with a much higher offer, know precisely where your limit is.

For a car or truck carrying a big incentive, one dealer or another should be ready to bargain. Don't go above a price that gives you half the dealer incentive—$500 below invoice in the example above.

Your maximum target price:_____

Consumer rebate, if any:_____
Subtract this amount from your target price.

This rebate is yours by right. It must not come into the negotiated price. Let the salesman know from the start you simply expect to subtract it at the end of negotiations.

Your selling price:_____
Target price minus any consumer rebate.

Sales Tax: _____
Your selling price times the percentage of state and local (if any) sales tax.

Freight charge:_____

Dealer advertising cost:_____
(Almost never negotiable, this is a regional fee. You must ask a local dealer or check the fine print in local ads to get the number.)

Your total cost:_____
Add your selling price, sales tax, freight charge, and dealer advertising:_____

This is the amount you must pay with cash or a loan. If you are leasing, it will be the first step in figuring your lease payments (see Chapter 10).

No-Dicker Planning

If you plan to deal with a one-price dealer and avoid haggling, you will not need to work fully through the worksheet. But you still will want to go as far as determining the dealer's invoice cost. Unless you are attracted enough by the Saturn mystique to pay the roughly 15% markup its dealers get (and

Saturn has among the most satisfied customers in the industry, according to the J. D. Power organization), you will want to be wary that you are not paying too much for the one-price convenience (see Chapter 9 for more details). A typical non-Saturn one-price dealer might be charging about 6% above invoice price. If the price on the one-price sticker is, say, invoice plus 10%, you probably want to do your no dickering at another dealer.

Then there is the General Motors so-called value pricing—practiced especially by its Oldsmobile division—which is like no-dicker pricing . . . but not exactly. These prices supposedly are no-dicker numbers. But unlike GM's real no-dicker division, Saturn, Oldsmobile and Chevrolet dealers often will cut the value prices if pushed. So with value pricing—as with standard pricing—figuring dealer cost can pay off.

Now you are in the enviable position of knowing exactly what you plan to pay for your new car. But unless you can pay with your own cash, it is time to go shopping for money.

Live and in Your Favorite Color

Sitting in and Driving New Cars without Getting Bogged Down in Negotiations

When you have a short list of cars or trucks you like that you also can afford, you need to check out the real thing. But you need to concentrate on the vehicle without the distraction of talking price at the same time. If your area has an auto show coming up anytime soon, that is the best place to start. It is worth the $15 or $20 admission ticket to be able to see all the new cars and trucks in one place and—usually—to be able to sit in them. While sitting in a car with the engine off may not seem like much of a thrill, you can learn a lot that way. For instance, you may find that the seats in a certain vehicle or the distance to the brake pedal and accelerator simply are not comfortable for you. If you are taller than six two or shorter than five two, this can be a major consideration. Or you may find that the design of the radio, heater, and other controls make it uncomfortable to reach for them from the driver's seat—an issue that can become a major annoyance on a long drive.

Visiting the auto show provides another advantage: You can look at a car or truck as long as you want and from any angle. Those breathtaking TV ads with your dream car zooming along the cliffs above the ocean or your favorite sport utility climbing a scenic mountain track only give you a quick look at the vehicle from its best angle. When you get a careful look at the manufacturer's show booth, you may realize the shape of that front fender bothers you or those taillights with the radical design spoil the look from the rear. If you find such design features really annoying, you can cross that car or truck off your list without ever having to discuss it with a salesman.

Useful as it is, though, the local auto show will not tell you what it feels like to take a particular car or truck out on the highway, over rough roads, or in city traffic. For that you must have a test drive. Dealers give lip service to providing pressure-free test drives. But in reality every dealer wants to sell every car today and get in new inventory. So it is up to you to establish when you arrive at a dealership that you are there only for a test drive and to repeat it politely but forcefully whenever necessary. Respond quickly and emphatically if the salesman or -woman starts with questions such as "What could I do to convince you to buy today?" The right answer: "Absolutely nothing. I am just beginning my research, and I haven't even decided what car to buy" (even if you think you have—nobody is going to give you a lie detector test).

While it would be ideal to take a test drive by yourself, dealers almost always insist that the salesman accompany you—partly out of an understandable concern that a solitary test driver could simply vanish with a new car. To avoid distraction, just tell the salesperson that you want to concentrate on the feel and sound of the car or truck and that you prefer not to talk while you are doing that. Try to insist on a drive of at least a half hour, and choose the route yourself. (The dealership's standard route may be designed either to avoid rough roads or other conditions that show off the car badly or simply to maneuver a relatively short drive.)

Think out your own test-drive route ahead of time, and try to include fast highway driving, rough pavement or railroad tracks, and noisy city traffic. If it is close enough, include part of the route that you actually drive to commute to work or to do errands.

Is the car or truck comfortable? Is it quiet? Move the driver's seat to various positions and see if you find several of them comfortable. You will want to move that seat during a long drive. Turn on the heater and then the air conditioner and switch the fan up to high. Is it quiet or is the whine annoying? Does the blowing air hit you too much in the face, or is it barely noticeable? Is it easy to change the direction and temperature of the air?

Turn on the radio. Switch to various stations you might play. Does the quality of sound measure up to your standards? If you plan to buy a compact disc player, bring along one or two of your favorite CDs and see how they sound.

If you have questions, ask the salesperson. Is this the top level of stereo available? How much more does the better CD player cost? But keep the discussions short and cut off anything that sounds like a sales pitch or negotiation.

When your test drive is through, take the salesperson's card, but do not leave your telephone number. If you want to talk to this dealership again, you can call them. Keep a notebook to record your impressions of your test drives and write them down as soon as you leave the dealership while they are fresh.

After a few test drives, you usually will start to have clear preferences. But if you simply feel that you need a whole day or more to be sure, try to rent the car model you are most interested in. Hertz specializes in Ford and Lincoln/Mercury rentals, Avis in General Motors, and Budget Rent-a-Car in Chrysler Corp. models. But these and other rental companies do have other models as well—including the biggest import lines such as Honda and Toyota. Except for sports cars, pickup trucks, and brand-new models, most cars, vans, and sport utilities are likely to be for rent somewhere in your town. A day or two of rental bills may turn out to be a cheap price for avoiding the wrong decision on what car, van, or sport utility you will buy.

CHAPTER 7

Shopping for Money

Getting a loan to finance your new car is much like disposing of your old car—the easiest way to do it is through your new-car dealer. But you usually will pay dearly for that convenience. As with a trade-in, mixing car loan details into new-car negotiations adds an element of confusion for you and increases the dealer's edge over you. Such a negotiation puts you in a spot where it is hard to determine your true costs. What you want is the opposite—to know your loan and other costs precisely even before you start negotiating about the car's price. For that reason, you want to shop for money before you shop for a car.

Willie Sutton was wrong: banks are not the only place where the money is anymore. Banks recently held about 43% of U.S. auto loans, according to figures from the Federal Reserve Board. Auto manufacturers' "captive" finance subsidiaries such as Ford Motor Credit and General Motors Acceptance Corporation hold about 20% of loans and credit unions and savings and loans another 25%.

A credit union—if you already belong to one or can figure out a way to become a member of one of these nonprofit organizations—typically charges one-half to one percentage point lower interest than bank car loans in the same area. A home-equity loan—in effect a second mortgage on your home—can be the cheapest loan of all once taxes are taken into account. Under current tax law, interest for a home-equity loan on your primary residence remains tax deductible, unlike all other forms of consumer interest. A home-equity loan can be an especially good deal if you already have an approved line of credit and will not need to pay any new fees to originate one.

Don't Shop Payments

When considering a loan (or a lease), your natural instinct is to think first about what your monthly payment will be. Resist that impulse. You must, of course, find out the monthly payments involved in a loan. But that number alone tells you very little about what you are paying for money. If you just mention a payment amount—such as $400 or below—to salesmen or finance specialists at a dealership, they have enormous leeway in structuring the loan, often to your disadvantage.

Find out the Price

Instead, shop for money the way you would clothes or food or anything else—by finding out the price. That price is the interest rate. With a few hours' work you should be able to find out which banks are offering the cheapest auto loan rates in your town at the time. It is well worth the trouble. The difference between the best and worst rates in a given area often will be three full percentage points—say, 8%–11%, although auto loan rates, like all interest rates, change constantly. Fortunately the banks with the best rates are likely to be bragging about it. Open your Friday or Sunday auto section in the local paper and look for the scattering of bank loan ads among the ones for cars and trucks. Also check the business section, which sometimes carries loan ads. The low promotional rates are likely to be in big type.

Start by calling the automotive finance departments at the banks running ads and see if there are any hidden restrictions on these loans. See what you need to do to get an application; they may be willing to fax it to you. Then keep calling a selection of large and medium-size banks to check their interest rates against the banks doing the advertising. Finally, call your own bank—especially if you have a so-called preferred banking relationship where you have agreed to keep minimum balances in certain accounts. Because of this relationship, you may get an auto loan break of about 0.5% points from your bank. The auto loan promotion at another bank may still produce the cheapest rate, however.

Make sure that in all discussions of interest rates, you are being quoted the annual percentage rate, or APR. State law in most states requires lenders to give you this number if asked. But if you do not insist, they sometimes will quote a lower, non-APR rate that camouflages origination or other fees charged for the loan. The APR takes such fees into account. Even so, check to see if a given bank is charging you an additional fee—perhaps $50 or $100—just for letting you submit a loan application. Such fees are becoming more common as banks are attempting to boost their fee income in this and all other areas.

Credit Unions:
Cheap Loans for Members Only

While credit unions typically offer cheaper car loan rates than banks, only members are eligible for these loans. So you may have trouble getting access to them unless you already are a credit union member. The ideal situation is where your company or your profession (college professors, state employees) has a credit union where you automatically become a member. If not, you may be able to get into a credit union anyway. Some credit unions will extend membership to siblings or even more distant relations of current members. So check with your brother, your sister, your aunt. If you belong to a union, a lodge, or other club or association, find out if it is affiliated with a credit union. Still other credit unions are based on a geographic area. If you happen to live in the right neighborhood, you automatically qualify for membership. To check out such possibilities, call 800-358-5710, where staffers from the Credit Union National Association will try to guide you to a credit union for which you might qualify.

Whether you are talking to bankers or credit union officials, arm yourself with a table of how monthly payments vary with the amount being borrowed, the interest rate, and the length of the loan. For a quick way to calculate the payments, have a look at the table that follows. While getting the lowest available interest rate will save money, keep in mind this important truth about loan payments: Cutting the amount you borrow reduces payments much more sharply than getting a moderately lower interest rate. Take this example: With a $15,000 loan at 9.5% for four years, your monthly payment will be $377. Cut that interest rate to 6% and your monthly payment goes down $25 to $352. But if you could borrow just $12,000 instead of $15,000 even at the higher 9.5%, your payment would drop $76 a month to $301. **So remember,** *the fastest way to cut your* *monthly payments is to buy a cheaper car or put up a bigger down payment.*

FIGURING YOUR PAYMENTS

The table below will allow you to determine your monthly auto loan payment at a variety of interest rates and for any dollar amount.

Simply take the dollar amount you wish to borrow, find the interest rate you can borrow your loan at, for the term you want, and multiply the figure listed by the dollar amount, in thousands, you wish to borrow.

For example, you wish to borrow $16,500 for 48 months at a 10% interest rate. Multiply the dollar amount (16.5 thousand) by the factor shown (25.36) to arrive at your monthly payment ($418.44).

	36 Months $ per 1000	48 Months $ per 1000	60 Months $ per 1000
11.00	32.73	25.84	21.74
10.75	32.62	25.72	21.61
10.50	32.50	25.60	21.49
10.25	32.38	25.48	21.37
10.00	32.26	25.36	21.24
9.75	32.14	25.24	21.12
9.50	32.03	25.12	21.00
9.25	31.91	25.00	20.87
9.00	31.79	24.88	20.75
8.75	31.68	24.76	20.63
8.50	31.56	24.64	20.51
8.25	31.45	24.53	20.39
8.00	31.33	24.41	20.27
7.75	31.22	24.29	20.15

	36 Months $ per 1000	48 Months $ per 1000	60 Months $ per 1000
7.50	31.10	24.17	20.03
7.25	30.99	24.06	19.91
7.00	30.87	23.94	19.80
6.75	30.76	23.83	19.68
6.50	30.64	23.71	19.56
6.25	30.53	23.59	19.44
6.00	30.42	23.48	19.33

Source: HSH Associates

Sometimes It's the Dealer's Deal

In some special cases, the dealer may after all have the best financing deal for you. If you have a history of credit problems but now have a marginally good credit rating, a dealer eager to sell a car may approve a loan for you more readily than a bank or credit union. But don't limit yourself to the dealer just because of past credit problems—especially if your credit has improved. Be frank about your situation with bank and credit union officers, and you may find that you qualify for a loan more easily than you thought—especially if the institution is in a period when it is trying to push new loans.

Even with a top credit rating you sometimes may want to take advantage of special low-interest dealer loans being promoted by the manufacturer—such as the 2.9% annual percentage rate recently offered by Ford on its new Taurus. But remember, what really cuts your payments is financing less. Promotional interest rates typically are offered as an option to a consumer rebate, and often, by taking that rebate and thus reducing the size of the loan, you will wind up with a better deal. By working with the following tables and those in the appendix, you can sort out which is to your advantage.

Financing a Used Car

The revolutionary change in the quality of used cars has resulted in a big change in used-car financing as well. As recently as the late 1980s lenders were worried that mechanical problems with used cars could threaten repayment of their loans. They fretted, as well, that people who bought used cars were likely to have poorer credit histories. So they charged from 2.0 to 2.5 percentage points more in interest rates than for similar new-car loans. But since most recent-model cars now are more durable and cars returning from leases provide a steady supply of prime used cars, banks and credit unions have become more confident in their used-car loans. New- and used-car buyers now have similar credit records. Now you have to pay just over one percentage point more in interest for a used-car loan than for a comparable new car loan. (A recent national average for used-car loans was 10.2%, compared with 8.97% for new-car financing.)

If you are looking for used-car financing, follow the same procedure as for a new car. Call local banks—and credit unions, if you belong to any—and get interest rate quotations for used-car loans. You probably will have to let the loan officer know what make and year used car or truck you intend to buy. Check the newspaper ads for new-car financing; you should be able to get a used-car quotation for a rate no more than 1.5 percentage points above the new-car rate.

With used cars even more than new cars, it is crucial not to focus on the level of monthly payments. Though things are changing with used cars, remnants of consumer gouging still can be found—and an unscrupulous dealer has maximum room to maneuver if you just talk about payments. President Keith Gumbinger of HSH Associates, a Butler, New Jersey, firm that compiles national statistics on loan interest rates, tells of an acquaintance who had bought a used car and financed it through the dealer after specifying monthly payments of $225. "I analyzed the loan and realized it carried a 22% interest rate," Gumbinger recalls. "We were able to get it refinanced at 7.5% and cut the payments by about one-third."

Whether you are eyeing a new or used vehicle, once you have discovered which bank or credit union is offering the lowest interest rate, make a formal loan application there. If you have a steady job and reasonably good credit history, you are likely to get loan approval, typically good up until a deadline date, perhaps two or three months away. Thus you can head out to shop for cars knowing that your financing is already set. You can focus your attention without distraction on getting the lowest possible price. If the car or truck you are considering carries a promotional low-interest-rate loan, you are still free to tap that if it is the better deal and just not use your preapproved loan. But knowing you have financing approved lets you weigh such a comparison with a clear head and without feeling any pressure. And if the same deal offers a choice to take a cash rebate rather than a low-interest loan from the manufacturer, you may find that your best deal is to use your original financing but take the rebate to trim the amount you are borrowing.

Once you have decided what type of vehicle you need, whether to buy new or used, and what models you can afford, gotten the prices on those models, and set up your financing, it is time to go shopping (or send someone to shop for you). In Part 2 we will help you hit the pavement on your way to a great deal.

PART 2

SHOPPING FOR THE BEST DEAL

CHAPTER 8

Hate Haggling? Then Hire Help: Buying Services Can Help You Get the Best Prices with Little Hassle

You say you hate the whole idea of haggling? That needn't keep you from buying a new car or truck. This chapter will guide you to the best places to get help in negotiating with auto dealers.

If you do dislike haggling, you have a lot of company. While Americans may scour the malls for discount prices, they nonetheless are used to buying everything from diapers to diamonds at the price marked on the display without bargaining about it. In a survey of recent new-car buyers by auto market researcher the Dohring Co., about 25% of respondents said they had avoided negotiating about price, and another 25% had negotiated but disliked the process. "Most people dislike negotiations, especially highly adversarial ones," says business consultant Alan Schoonmaker, author of the book *Negotiate to Win*.

"We rarely haggle about anything." But while hagglers may not have more fun, they usually get the best deals on cars.

That is true because auto dealers have clung tenaciously to a haggling system that has more in common with a Marrakesh bazaar than the Mall of America. Though the system is finally starting to change, haggling still reigns. A dealer thus retains the freedom to charge the highest possible price for a car or truck he or she can negotiate with a given customer. Those who do not negotiate hard risk becoming one of those customers who fatten dealer profits by paying more for a given model of car or truck than tougher shoppers. While you may hate haggling, you also hate hearing from your neighbor that he bought the same car for $500 or even $1,000 less.

So as you think about buying a new car, you'll want to choose early among three alternatives:

- You will know the dealer's costs so well and have such a firm strategy that you will have the confidence to negotiate the deal yourself. (See Chapter 12 for details on negotiating strategy and tactics.)
- You will avoid negotiations entirely by selecting a Saturn or another brand sold by a dealer who has adopted no-dicker, one-price selling. (See Chapter 9.)
- You will pay someone to do the shopping and negotiating for you (see following).

TEST YOUR HAGGLE READINESS

Your answers to the questions below will help you determine how you should shop for a car.

1. Have you been involved in negotiations in the past, either in your job (perhaps setting prices with suppliers) or as part of community activities (such as determining charges for the caterer at a fund-raising event)?_____

2. Do you find the competition involved in negotiations stimulating, even fun?_____

3. Do you have time, at least a couple of weekends, to play off competing dealers against one another until you get the best price?_____

If you answered "Yes" to at least two of these questions, you may want to consider negotiating your own car deal. About half of the new car buyers in the Dohring survey had negotiated their own deals and had liked the transaction. The report notes that dealers are trying harder in recent years to "improve customers' purchase satisfaction." Translation: The old adversarial, intimidating sales style is not as common in auto showrooms as it used to be. But it still exists. And if you encounter a high-pressure full-court press to "Buy *TODAY*," use your ultimate weapon: walk out and don't go back.

Now try these questions:

1. Do you find negotiating so unpleasant that you might even pay a higher price than you intend in order to end the process?_____

2. Is saving time important enough to you that minimizing the time spent car shopping is a major goal?_____

3. Is it a top priority to feel that you got the lowest available price?_____

Answer truthfully now. This is not a pass-fail test, where tough characters who like negotiating get extra points. We are trying to help you make an honest assessment of your most effective way to shop for a new car or truck. If you answered "Yes" to the first two questions but "No" to the third, or if you have no strong feelings about knowing you got an extraordinarily good deal, you might consider a one-price dealer. The shopping experience is likely to be a pleasant one with no haggling, and everyone who buys the same vehicle near the same time as you will be getting the same price.

But if saving time and getting the lowest possible price are top priorities for you, you need to hire somebody to do the negotiating—or at least take bids—for you. *Hiring help lets you avoid most of the hassle but still take advantage of the reality that hard negotiators get the best prices.* Here, starting with the full-service (and therefore the most expensive) operations and moving through the less expensive services that give you partial assistance with your auto deal, are the best places to hire help for car shopping.

Full Service

If your idea of a good shopping experience is just showing up at the dealer to pay, do the paperwork, and take your new car or truck home, then you may find the $250–$450 per vehicle fee of an auto-buying service well worth the price. The best of these services work only for you and get bids from competing dealers to negotiate the lowest possible price; they do not have profit-sharing or other arrangements for payments from dealers. About 30 such services across the country have such fee-only setups. If you are uncertain of the status of a buyers' service you are considering, check with the trade group National Association of Buyers' Agents (800-517-2277), which checks to make sure a service is fee-only before admitting it to membership.

Among the best-established national services is AutoAdvisor in Seattle (800-326-1976; $335 for factory orders, $359 to shop among dealers for the vehicle you want). CarSource in Larkspur, California (800-517-2277; $375 for most vehicles), is run by Linda Lee Goldberg, who also is president of the trade association. Automobile Consumer Services in Cincinnati (800-223-4882) charges $249 for a factory order and $295 to find a car in stock.

Using a buying service will not save you from doing your homework. You still must do the research to know precisely what vehicle you want before calling a buying service. Then you let the service know within what area you would consider picking up the car ("Within 100 miles of Chicago," for instance, or "anywhere in the Dallas–Ft. Worth area"). But once you have given them a precise order, such services deal with the fleet departments of dealerships—meaning the dealer can avoid a commission to one of its sales people on your vehicle. Unless you are a black-belt negotiator, the pros from the buying service are likely to get a better deal than you would have on your own (offset, of course, by the amount of their fee). They always are aware of any dealer incentives being offered on the vehicle you want to buy and can negotiate to get a large percentage of that incentive as savings for you.

Dealing with such services does not provide the instant gratification of finding a car you want on a dealer's lot and buying it the same day. But such impulse buying isn't very likely to get you a good deal. If you are patient enough to wait for up to eight weeks, putting in a factory order is the surest way to get exactly the model and color you want and often will produce the lowest price as well if you are buying a General Motors, Ford, or Chrysler vehicle. Most Japanese and European makes, however, do not take factory orders, and thus you must get a car from dealer inventory. Patience is necessary even if you are ordering from inventory. If a service has promised to find you a car or truck within four weeks, it often will take most of that time to deliver. You sometimes can pay extra for more speed. AutoAdvisor, for instance, promises two-week delivery for $569.

If you plan to use a buying service, you need to arrange financing on your own first from a bank or credit union. While occasionally these services are able to arrange leasing deals, it is not their specialty. As their name suggests, buying services work best when you plan to buy the car. Once you have placed an order, the service takes bids from within the area you have stipulated. When the service has located your car or truck at what it believes is the lowest available price, its people call you with this offer. If you agree on the terms, the dealership will hold that specific vehicle until you come to pay for it and pick it up.

Competing Bids

If you want to pay lower fees but still get competing bids through an organization that takes no money from dealers, there is an alternative. Of course, for less money, you do more of the work yourself. Car Bargains (800-475-7283) charges $150 per vehicle to get competing bids from at least five dealers in your region. You tell Car Bargains what car you are looking for—say, a Toyota Camry LE four-door sedan or a Jeep Grand Cherokee Laredo four-wheel drive. At this stage of the process, you do not have to get more specific—such as stipulating whether you want your sport utility with a compact disc player.

In about two weeks you will get a package from Car Bargains (you can get it by fax or express delivery at no extra cost, if you want), first setting out the MSRP or list price and dealer's invoice price both for the basic model and various options. Accompanying that list will be bids from various dealers, which will be couched in terms of amount over or (occasionally) under invoice price. Let's say a dealer bids $200 over invoice and at that time, a Camry LE had a list price of $19,778 and a dealer invoice of $17,146. If you wanted to add antilock brakes to that car, the invoice price for that option was $902 for a total invoice price of $18,048. So the dealer's price to you would be $18,248. Unfortunately there still are some other nonnegotiable items to be added in, which would have been stipulated on the dealer's bid. At this time the destination charge on the Camry was $420. And the dealer's advertising fee—levied on each dealer for regional advertising—might run $200. This item varies by area but unfortunately is nonnegotiable. Thus the total invoice price would be $18,698 and the dealer's bid $18,898. Of course you also still must add on state sales tax and fees for your license plates.

Unlike a full-fledged buying service, however, Car Bargains has not gone looking for a specific vehicle equipped just as you want and perhaps in a certain color. So now you must call the contact stipulated at the low-bidding dealer (often the fleet manager) and see if he has the car you want. If he does not, he may be able to locate it at another local dealer and negotiate a swap to get it for you. If that fails, he could put in a factory order if you are willing to wait up to eight weeks and are buying a Detroit product. Some dealers stipulate in their bids a separate, often slightly lower, price for a factory order.

Thus with Car Bargains you may have a harder time finding the exact car or truck you want than with a more expensive buying service. But you still know you got a price produced by competitive bidding that lets the dealer avoid a sales commission. Tests by **MONEY** magazine and others have shown the low bid from Car Bargains will often be among the lowest prices any service can produce. And the lower fee saves an additional $100–$200 versus the more expensive buying services.

Dealer Referral

A third type of car-buying service offered through local American Automobile Association (AAA) auto clubs and discount warehouse store chains charges no fee beyond your annual membership dues but are unlikely to get you the lowest possible price. That is because, unlike buying services and Car

Bargains, these operations do not seek out competing bids. Instead they refer you to just one dealer in your area for each make (one Chevrolet, one Honda, etc.). In return, the dealer agrees to sell to members at a fixed price below the MSRP and pays the sponsoring organization for being included on the referral list.

The parent organizations set overall price guidelines but do not enforce them on every individual deal. Sam's Club, the most forthright of the sponsors, says it aims for its dealers to average transaction prices of about 1% over the dealer invoice price on domestic makes and 3% over invoice on import nameplates. The other sponsors, Price/Costco (through its Price Club and Costco stores) and the AAA, decline to specify their price guidelines.

In a **MONEY** magazine shopping test, we found that in nine of 10 comaparisons in three cities, Car Bargains beat the prices being offered by dealers referred through Sam's Club and Price/Costco. To use these services you first need to join the AAA (typical annual dues about $50) or one of the warehouse shopping clubs ($25–$35). Then you get a printed list of dealers or call an 800 number for a referral to the dealer nearest you who handles the car or truck you want. As with other services, you are given the name of a specific contact to call at that dealership. But **MONEY** magazine correspondents found a wide variation in service from various dealerships in the warehouse plans. Some were quick to respond to calls and clear and specific on what the fixed price would be either over the phone or, in some cases, in a required in-person visit. Others were slow to respond to messages, vague about the prices, and, in one case, seemingly trying to negotiate in what was supposed to be a fixed-price deal.

On the World Wide Web, a service called Auto-by-Tel (available through Edmund's price site: http://www.edmunds.com) provides a similar service. You post the details of the vehicle you are looking for, and Auto-by-Tel will have a dealer contact you. Like the AAA and warehouse clubs, however, this does not produce competing bids. Auto-by-Tel has one affiliated dealer for each brand that pays it for referrals in a given geographical area.

Bottom line: While the auto club and discount warehouse services and Internet referral will not usually get you the best possible price, they will beat what you will pay if you are a reluctant, poor negotiator or if you have not done your homework about dealer cost and other details. And if you are impatient but flexible about color and options, such a dealer referral may let you buy a car within a day or two from the dealer's stock or a swap with another local dealer—much more quickly than a regular buying service or Car Bargains.

Local Brokers

In many cities local auto brokers advertise in the Yellow Pages and elsewhere, offering to do your shopping for you. While some of them do in fact deliver good deals, be wary. Because these brokers, unlike buying services, take title to the car and then resell it to you, the possibility of fraud is higher. Since you do not deal directly with the dealer, problems also can emerge in showing that you are the initial owner for the warranty or, if you have problems, for the state lemon law. If you are considering a local broker, check with your state attorney general's office and the Better Business Bureau to see if the broker has any complaints outstanding against him. (Brokers are not available everywhere. In Texas and Maryland, for instance, dealers have lobbied successfully to have the state legislature ban them.) If the broker checks out, ask him to go over the warranty and lemon law situation with you.

Another problem with local brokers is that they typically take money both from clients and dealers. They may charge you a fee of $50 or $100. At the same time, they are getting paid by the dealer to bring in sales. So competitive bidding is unlikely, and the fee to the broker pads your price.

Nonetheless, local brokers sometimes will beat the prices of the dealer referral services. And they usually are willing to discuss a variety of car models with you and suggest on which one you are likely to get the best price. You can feel a little more confident if you find the broker through a referral. For instance, credit unions often keep an approved list of local car brokers.

Now, That's a Good Deal

In deciding whether to do your own auto shopping or hire some help, you simply must determine what is the most important to you: what combination of price savings vs. the hassle of shopping is your perfect balance. It does not matter if you do it alone or with help. If you buy or lease the car or truck, sport utility, or van you really want and you do it for the price you had budgeted and planned to pay, then you got a good deal.

CHAPTER 9

One Price but Not the Highest Price

Would you like to shop in a showroom where the salespeople answer your questions but do not push you to come to a decision? Where there is no haggling over price and where you can be sure that the next customer to buy the same model will not get a lower price? Then you may want to shop at a one-price dealer. The trend of switching to one-price selling by dealerships has slowed since its peak in the early 1990s, but there are about 1,000 or more dealers nationwide who follow this approach.

Although one-price showrooms are a lot more pleasant than the traditional car-buying experience, that does not mean you want to let down your guard. You can just as readily add to your costs with a poor trade-in or high-cost financing at a no-dicker dealer as at a traditional haggle-happy shop. This chapter will help you wake up and smell the cappuccino in the dealer's coffee bar and make sure that one price is not the highest price.

One-Price Test

Test yourself on these additional questions to see if you may be a candidate for one-price shopping.

1. When you shop for a television or stereo, do you tend to take the best price you can find after shopping one or two stores without taking those offers to the chain whose ads scream "We'll Beat Any Price?"_____

2. Do you find clipping out coupons and carrying them to the supermarket more trouble than the savings are worth?

_____

3. Will you shop at stores like Nordstrom's, where the service is especially courteous and attentive even if the prices are a little higher than those of some competitors?_____

If you answered "Yes" to at least two of these questions, you may be a candidate for one-price car shopping.

Saturn has proved that some car customers care a lot more about how they are treated while buying their car and in the service department afterward than they do about how much profit the dealer is making. Saturn's absolutely-no-dicker selling price is nearly 15% above the dealer's invoice price—more than twice the 7.1% average profit by dealers on all new cars sold. But by focusing strictly on consumer satisfaction, Saturn has delivered it. In the annual Consumer Satisfaction Index compiled by auto research firm J. D. Power & Co., Saturn has been at or near the top of the list in recent years, rubbing fenders with luxury nameplates like Lexus and Infiniti, whose top-of-the-line models cost three times as much as a Saturn. (Satisfaction may be increased by the Saturn price level—mostly below $15,000.)

The whole approach pays off with Saturn owners like Kathy

Nolan, who works for the U.S. Post Office in New Jersey in the division that investigates violations of postal regulations. "I had been to other dealers, and at Saturn it was much more relaxed, with no stress. I did not feel I was dealing with a prototype car salesman," she recalls. "And I knew that the next customer who came in was not going to get the car for $1,000 less."

But Saturn and its 15% profit margin are a special case. In the division General Motors started from scratch, Saturn top executives were able to make the fixed price stick by limiting the number of franchises so that a customer at one Saturn dealer could not drive just down the road to a competitor to try to get a cheaper price. Dealers who adopted the one-price, low-pressure approach for other brands—often Saturn dealers who owned other franchises as well—had a big disadvantage. Unlike Saturn customers, their shoppers could take their fixed selling price a few miles away to a competitor, who often would beat that price. As a result, about half the 2,000 dealers who tried one-price selling in the early 1990s have gone back to their old haggling ways. The remaining 1,000 or so dealers (out of 15,000 total) who take the one-price approach average a 5%–6% markup over invoice, estimates consultant Bob Fitzharris of J. D. Power.

The fast-expanding CarMax chain of superstores has brought new attention to one-price selling, especially when Chrysler granted the company a new-car franchise to add to their previously all-used operation. The parent corporation of CarMax, electronics retailer Circuit City, believes cars can be sold like television sets, with different brands all sold together and consumers readily able to check out the selection—starting with pictures on a video screen followed by an on-the-spot inspection of particular cars that interest you.

Industry analysts note, however, that one-price selling fits more easily with used cars than new. With a new Taurus, Camry, or Jeep Cherokee, the customer can look at virtually the same vehicle at a nearby showroom and bargain for a lower price. Since each used car is unique in its color, mileage, and condition, you won't easily find the same thing if you go price shopping. "If you are looking at a two-year-old dark green Cherokee equipped just the way you want it, you may not find another one anywhere nearby," notes Power analyst Fitzharris.

But owners of two so-called auto malls in the Midwest, each of which offers a dozen or more new-car brands, believe that customers like to buy new cars this way as well. At Mauro Auto Mall in Kenosha, Wisconsin, and Lujack's Northpark Auto Plaza in Davenport, Iowa, salespeople are not paid more if they sell a high-profit vehicle. Shoppers can compare one brand to another right on the spot and buy at fixed prices.

These operations also concentrate on customer comfort. The Mauro mall, for instance, has a child care center that will look after the kids while parents shop, plus free coffee and soft drinks if you want to sit down and talk over the deal with your spouse. If you are bringing back a vehicle you already bought for service, Mauro provides a shuttle bus for shopping at a nearby factory outlet mall and a beeper to let you know when your car is ready.

No Escaping Homework

Remember, buying a new car or truck is a big purchase. Expecting friendly and courteous, no-hassle service at a one-price dealer does not mean you want to avoid doing your homework. Before you go:

- Look up the invoice price of the vehicles that interest you in a price guide or on the World Wide Web (see Chapter 5). If the no-haggle price is set more than 8% above the invoice price, try a different one-price dealer where you can likely find a better no-dicker price.
- If you have a vehicle to trade in, determine its value in advance. Even at a no-haggle dealer, you may be able to

negotiate the trade upward if you think the dealership offer is not high enough. Check your library or ask your insurance agent or bank loan officer to show you the *NADA Official Used Car Guide* (see page 58) to get some idea of the valuations dealers will be using. Look at the used-car ads in your local paper or specialized classified ad publication. See how cars like yours seem to be priced. And if your car or truck is less than four years old and thus worth a sizable trade-in, you may want to take the trouble to visit the used-car operations of one or two dealers that sell the same make as yours to see what they will offer for your old vehicle. You then can use that standard when discussing trade-in with the one-price dealer—even if you are shopping for a Saturn.

• As with any dealer, shop for a loan before you shop for a car. You are likely to get a lower interest rate from a bank or, especially, a credit union than at the dealership, unless the car you are shopping for happens to carry a low promotional loan rate from the manufacturer.

Dealing with a one-price dealer is likely to be a lot more pleasant and comfortable than shopping at a traditional bazaar-style dealership. But even so, it is still up to you to be vigilant that you are not giving the dealer money you could be saving.

Value Pricing

Saturn's success with one-price selling has led one of its sister divisions at General Motors, Oldsmobile, to try a similar approach. Olds sets a "value price" for its models below the traditional sticker price and about 5%–6% above dealer invoice cost. But Oldsmobile does not have Saturn's advantage of a limited number of dealerships that preclude nearby competition.

So in the real world, Oldsmobile's supposedly fixed prices are usually negotiable. The same is true at sister division Chevrolet, where a handful of models are value priced.

Luxury car maker Infiniti, a subsidiary of Nissan, is taking another route. Infiniti executives have announced that while they would not go to fixed-price selling, they would cut back their list price closer to an average transaction price. As a result, Infiniti MSRPs are dropping from a whopping 17% over dealer invoice—fairly typical for luxury cars—to about 6% above invoice. Company executives say that their research showed Infiniti shoppers were annoyed by what they saw as the inflated MSRPs on the cars but "don't see one price as totally legitimate. Some price negotiation still is important in the luxury market." So if you are a hard bargainer, you probably can get an Infiniti for slightly below the new asking level, perhaps 4% above the dealer's invoice.

CHAPTER 10

Leasing: Through the Looking Glass

Auto leasing is a strange, jargon-filled world, and the dealers like it that way. That obscurity often has helped them build high profits into lease deals. At first it is hard to understand what someone selling you a lease is talking about, let alone what the deal is going to cost you.

But once you break through and master the jargon, you can analyze a lease deal like any other transaction. This chapter will show you how to do that analysis.

If you are a leasing candidate, by now you probably know who you are. As laid out in the leasing test in Chapter 4, you might be a leaser if you tend to trade for a new car every four years or less, want to avoid coming up with a down payment, typically take good care of your vehicle, and hate the idea of disposing of your old car.

But if the concept of leasing sounds attractive, you still have to spot the real-world good deals—many of which are subsidized leases from the manufacturers rather than from banks, credit unions, or other institutions.

The first step is to understand what leasing is and is not.

The Basics

When you lease a car or truck, you do not buy it, nor do you rent it. The leasing company holds the title to the vehicle. (Recently, "captive" finance companies owned by manufacturers such as Ford Motor Credit and General Motors Acceptance Co. held 42% of leases; independent finance companies such as General Electric Capital had 30%, banks 25%, and credit unions 3%.) You are paying for the difference between the value of the car when the lease begins and the estimated value at the end of your lease. Seen another way, your lease payments cover the depreciation on the car, plus interest charges, plus sales taxes and fees, if any.

The starting value of the vehicle, the equivalent of the purchase price, is known as the **capitalized cost.** The equivalent of the interest rate is called the **money factor** and usually is expressed in decimal fractions, such as .0037. (To get an annual interest rate, multiply by 2400; .0037 equals an 8.88% annual rate.) The fixed value for the vehicle at the end of the lease is called the **residual value.** Most leases also give you the option to buy the car or truck at lease end, usually for the residual value or a price close to it.

You can reduce your monthly lease payments by getting a lower capitalized cost, a higher residual value, or both. When manufacturers subsidize lease deals on slow-moving models, they often do so by inflating the residual value. When there is no special lease deal, vehicles that hold a high resale value make better leasing candidates than those that depreciate more rapidly. Higher resale, or residual, value means lower payments. Examples of high-resale makes and models include Saturn, Honda, Toyota, Mercedes-Benz, and most minivans and sport utilities.

Getting Information

Dealers want you to talk only about monthly payments. You want to zero in on the other, more interesting details. In the past, dealers often resisted discussing the capitalized cost or purchase price equivalent—especially if they were basing the lease on the full manufacturer's suggested retail price or an even higher number. Now that is changing. Some large states, including New York, New Jersey, Florida, and Washington, now require that the capitalized cost be disclosed. Elsewhere, the major manufacturers' finance companies and others who generate 75% of U.S. leases have voluntarily agreed to disclose this number. And the Federal Reserve Board, which regulates consumer leases, has released new rules effective in October 1997 that require auto lease companies to disclose the capitalized cost.

You still may have to push aggressively for the information you need. But if a salesman or dealership manager repeatedly refuses to tell you details of the deal, just leave and tell them you are headed for a dealership where you don't have to guess about the terms of the lease. But you can get started finding out what you need in the fine print of the leasing ads. Open the weekend auto section in your local paper and see if the lease ads cover any car or truck model that is on your wish list. Then start pulling out details. For instance, a recent Nissan leasing ad was trumpeting in the headline that leases for three of its models featured "nothing down," a good start.

The lease on the Nissan Altima GXE called for a term of 39 months with payments of $239 a month. Dropping down into the fine print at the bottom of the ad, you could pick up these additional facts with a little calculation:

- The Altima lease was based on a $19,698 sticker price minus a dealer discount of $3,335, equaling a capitalized cost of $16,363.

- "Purchase option at the end of the lease for a price of $10,834." In most cases, this is the residual value. But when you go to the dealer, double-check this. Do not accept a purchase option higher than the residual value, thus building in potential profit for the dealer. In this ad the implied residual value is 55% of the sticker price versus a projected value of about 47% shown in industry reference *Automotive Lease Guide.* Nissan clearly is inflating the residual value to subsidize this lease and reduce payments. ***Such inflated residual value is the clearest signal of a subsidized lease and likely good deal.***

As is often the case in these ads, the money factor is not spelled out. And at least until the Federal Reserve starts enforcing its new regulations, that is the figure you also are likely to have the hardest time squeezing out of the dealer. But we will show you in the following worksheet how to figure that number if you have all the other factors. (In a bargain lease deal, the implied interest rate in the lease often will be lower than the then-current interest rate for auto loans, although it may not be sharply lower than market rates if the lease already carries an inflated residual value.)

THE INTEREST RATE

1. Enter the capitalized cost:_____

2. Enter the residual value:_____

3. Subtract the residual value (2.) from the capitalized cost(1.). Enter the result here:_____. This equals the depreciation for the life of the lease.

4. Enter the lease term (in months):_____

5. Divide the depreciation (3.) by the term (4.):_____. This is the monthly depreciation.

6. Enter the monthly payment:_____

7. Subtract the monthly depreciation (5.) from the monthly payment (6.). Enter result here:_____. This is the monthly finance charge.

8. Add capitalized cost (1.) plus residual value (2). Enter result here:_____

9. Divide result in (7.) by result in (8.):_____

10. Multiply the result in (9.) by 2,400:_____. This is your approximate annual interest rate in whole numbers (6.25 equals 6.25%, for example).

Using Your Computer

There is a simpler way to do these calculations if you are adept with a computer and feel it is worth the cost. Getting such software makes sense especially if you expect you are likely to lease a car not only now, but again in a few years. The *Expert Lease* program for Windows from Chart Software (800-418-8450) lets you analyze lease deals easily as well as compare the total cost of buying versus leasing a given vehicle. For $99.95 the package also gives you data on residual values from *Automotive Lease Guide* as well as list prices and dealer's invoice prices for all new vehicles. You get one free update of that data within 12 months. If you buy the software and then are considering leasing again in two or three years, you can get a fresh data update for $29.95.

If you do not want to invest in software but do want to be able to check residual value in leases against the industry estimate of market value, Chart Software will sell you a single copy of *Automotive Lease Guide* for $12.50.

Avoid the Biggest Mistakes

If you have spotted a lease deal that looks attractive, stop before moving ahead and double-check that you are avoiding these pitfalls, mistakes that people frequently make with leases that can cause them trouble or cost them money later.

• **Think twice before taking a lease that lasts longer than the car's warranty.**

For the major manufacturers now, that usually means a three-year warranty period. To double-check the warranty on vehicles that interest you, ask a dealer, look in manufacturer's brochures, or check the manufacturer's home page on the World Wide Web (see Chapter 6). "Imagine how you would feel if you paid $1,000 repair bill and then had to turn the car back in a few months," cautions Art Spinella, vice president and general manager of CNW Marketing/Research in Bandon, Oregon, a firm that follows leasing trends.

• **Never accept a lease with an allowance for less (or more) mileage than you need.**

Leases are based on maximum allowable mileage, and charge penalties if you rack up more. If commuting or other trips put 15,000 miles a year on your odometer, be sure you are not getting a lease that allows only 12,000 miles a year—increasingly a typical number.

For instance, the Nissan Altima lease cited earlier imposes a 15-cents-per-mile charge for everything over the equivalent of 12,000 miles a year. On the other hand, don't take a 15,000 annual mileage allowance if you know you will use only 10,000. Lower mileage ought to mean lower payments. And many lease companies are willing to alter the mileage limits—especially if you stay at or below 15,000 miles a year.

• **Do not forget to protect yourself against theft or serious collision loss early in the lease.**

If the vehicle is stolen or totaled, your insurance will pay just the depreciated market value at that time. Within the first two years that may well be less than the balance you owe on your lease. **Gap insurance** will pay the difference. Expect to get coverage for about $300 for the length of the lease; most major leasing companies offer such coverage. This is one of the few times when an add-on item being sold by the dealer is worth the price. You especially need gap insurance with a subsidized manufacturer's lease with inflated residual value. That payment-lowering maneuver makes it almost certain that the insurance payment will fall below the lease balance early in the lease.

• **Most of all, never take a lease based on sticker price.**

Even with the new requirements for disclosure, dealers and leasing companies will still find some easy marks who will sign up for high-cost leases because the monthly payments sound attractively low. Don't be one of those high-profit customers. If you plan to lease, start out with price research just as if you were a potential buyer (see Chapter 6). Know the dealer's cost and your own target level above that cost. And plan to negotiate on the capitalized cost.

Try Negotiating

Even if you are responding to an ad for a subsidized lease where a reduction from sticker price is already built in, try negotiating anyway. With such deals, the residual value and the money factor—or interest rate—are preset by the manufacturer. But the dealer is still free to negotiate the capitalized cost—accepting less profit if he is eager to conclude a deal. Your chance of getting a further reduction is especially good if you have determined that the car or truck in question carries an incentive payment from the manufacturer to the dealer (Chapter 6).

But in the case of some of the most aggressively subsidized lease deals, you may not be able to knock down the capitalized cost further. For instance, the Nissan Altima deal cited earlier carries a capitalized cost of $16,363—7% below the dealer's invoice cost of $17,533. Even with the 2% holdback a dealer typically gets from Nissan, this lease is based on a capitalized cost below the actual net dealer cost. His profit most likely is based on hitting manufacturer's sales targets and collecting a dealer incentive of up to 7% of the list price. Instead of trying to beat down the capitalized cost on a heavily subsidized deal like this one, save your energy to be vigilant against any fees that might be added on to your bill.

If your fancy has settled on a car, truck, or van where no special lease is being offered, however, then negotiating the capitalized cost is imperative. When you get to the dealer, do not mention leasing. Start negotiating the price on the car just as if you were buying. When you have reached a negotiated price, then bring up leasing. Still do not make clear that you prefer to lease. Say you need to compare buying and leasing alternatives and want to see what lease payments would be at the price you just agreed upon. As with any lease deal, insist on knowing the residual value and all other details. Know the market residual value in advance to make sure the dealer is not slipping in a low-ball residual value to make up for the low price you just negotiated.

If you are going in for such everything-on-the-table negotiations to lease a vehicle, you need to know in advance what your payments will be if you hit your target price on the capitalized cost. You probably will not be able to discover in advance what money factor your dealer's lease is using. But for your calculations, assume it matches the current auto loan rate in your area (see Chapter 7). Then plug your numbers into this worksheet.

MONTHLY PAYMENTS

1. Enter your target price as capitalized cost:_____
Estimate your target level starting with dealer's invoice cost and adding on 2% for cars with an MSRP of less than $20,000, 4% for more expensive vehicles. Add any expected acquisition fee. Subtract trade-in value reduced by loan payoff amount, if any. If the lease requires a down payment (capitalized cost reduction), subtract that amount also.

2. Enter expected residual value:_____
Use *Automotive Lease Guide* value for an estimate until you learn what value dealer lease contract is using.

3. Subtract residual value (2.) from capitalized cost (1.). Enter result here:_____

4. Enter the expected term of the lease (in months):_____

5. Divide the amount in (3.) by the term (4.). Enter result here:_____

6. Add capitalized cost (1.) to residual (2.). Enter result here: _____

7. Enter money factor here:_____
If you have annual interest rate in whole numbers, divide by 2,400 to get the money factor. Multiply result in line 6 by money factor (7.). Enter result:_____

8. Add result in line 5 to the result in line 7. Enter monthly payment here:_____

9. To account for sales tax, multiply the result in line 8 by 1 plus the sales tax rate. Enter payment with tax here:_____
(For example: If the sales tax rate is 6%, multiply by 1.06;

if it is 7.5%, multiply by 1.075; if it is 10%, multiply by 1.10. *This method works in most states, but a few states tax lease payments differently. Check with your accountant or the state tax department to be sure.)*

Watch Those Fees

The auto dealers' instinct to tack on miscellaneous fees wherever possible does not vanish with a switch from buying to leasing. In fact, it is often easier to camouflage such fees in a lease contract by incorporating them into monthly payments. You cannot avoid paying the state license fees and sales tax. You may be asked to pay for the license up front, but the sales tax likely will be built into the monthly payments. But other fees may be more avoidable. A so-called acquisition fee when the contract is signed starts around $100 but lately has been creeping up as high as $450. Disposition fees of similar amounts may be charged at the end of the lease, especially if you do not opt to buy the vehicle. A dealer eager to lease may be willing to reduce or eliminate these fees. Your leverage ought to be especially strong when dealing with an attractive manufacturer-subsidized lease like the Nissan example cited earlier, where the basic elements of the lease are preset for all dealers. Shop two or three dealers for Nissan or whatever brand is offering the lease, and tell each you are going to lease where you can get the lowest fees.

Probably the most contentious fee associated with leasing (and a major negative for some people) are the fees that the dealer can levy at the end of the lease for "excess wear and tear." As you readily see, this is a vague and subjective term that can be interpreted differently by different inspectors with different instructions. In general, the "captive" finance companies of Ford, GM, and Chrysler and the import brands will be a bit more lenient in such inspections because they want you to lease the same make again. Banks and independent finance companies, who back leases for a wide range of makes, are likely to be stricter. Your best defense against problems with excess wear and tear, however, comes before you have ever driven the car one mile. Try to make sure the lease spells out in as much detail as possible what constitutes excess wear and tear—then pay attention to it during the lease. Some items that almost always will be charged for are nearly bald or mismatched tires and missing or dented parts—including chrome strips and other essentially decorative components. If the car had hubcaps when you got it, it must have four hubcaps when you turn it in.

Even if your lease clearly spells out what condition your vehicle must be in, you may want to know before the final day of the lease whether you are likely to owe excess wear and tear penalties. The answer to that question may help determine whether you want to turn back the leased car or exercise your option to buy it. A month or more before the lease ends, call the dealer and try to arrange for an early inspection. If the dealership agrees, clean up the vehicle and take it in. If, for instance, numerous dents and scratches are going to result in a $1,000 fee, you might consider whether avoiding that fee might make it worth buying your leased car instead of leasing a new one.

Do I Want to Buy It?

Conventional wisdom holds that if you think you might want to buy the car at the end of the lease, you should avoid a lease with inflated residual value because that also is inflating your potential purchase price. This frequently is not true, says Charles Hart, president of Chart Software, which sells *Expert Lease* software. By avoiding inflated residual values, you are missing out on most of the best lease deals, he points out. And if you can show at the end that the market value of the vehicle is far less than the amount stipulated in the lease contract, the dealer may be willing to negotiate on the purchase price.

As the end of the lease nears, start out by checking the current value of your vehicle in the *NADA Official Used Car Guide* or in *Edmund's Used Cars Prices & Ratings.* Then take your leased car or truck to a few used-car dealers and see what they will offer for it. (See Chapter 5 on valuing your trade-in.) Armed with the knowledge of the wholesale value of your car, start negotiating with the dealer. Start by bidding that wholesale value. If you really want to keep the vehicle, you may move a little higher during negotiations, but don't pay the retail price listed in the price guides. That is what the dealer would ask another buyer after he had reconditioned the car. The dealer may see the attraction in the deal you are offering. "If he takes the car back, he has to clean it up and either send it to an auction or put it on his used-car lot," says Charles Hart. "If he makes a deal with you, he just gets a check for the car."

One caution: Such discount offers to buy may not work with vehicles that are hot sellers on the used-car lot, such as Ford Explorers and most other sport utilities. But those same vehicles are less likely than others to carry promotional leases with inflated residual values in the first place.

Leasing Used Cars

As manufacturers and other leasing companies watched the swift growth of leasing and used-car sales, they eventually concluded that they should try leasing used cars. That combination also is producing swift expansion. Art Spinella of CNW Marketing/Research estimates that one million used vehicles will be leased in 1997—up from just 150,000 in 1995. While leasing a two- or three-year-old car seems like a dicey proposition on the face of it, Spinella argues that under certain conditions it can be a good deal for the consumer. He points out that the best candidates for used-car leasing are domestic makes, where the biggest depreciation happens in the first two to three years (in most import makes the decline is steadier from year to year). For instance, even a new Saturn SL2, which holds its value well compared with competitors', will be worth 68% of its list price after two years and 51% after four years, according to *Automotive Lease Guide.* Based on a 1996 model price of $12,295, that means someone leasing that Saturn for the first two years of its life would be basing the lease on depreciation of $3,935, while the decline the second two years would be just $2,090. If the annual interest rate used was 9%, that would mean monthly payments on a two-year new-car lease without sales tax of $241.41. But on the two-year used-car lease, before taxes, the payment would be just $141.95.

Spinella and others advise that the best candidates for used-car leasing are the brands such as Saturn, where the manufacturer has a used-car certification program. (Others include Infiniti, Jaguar, Lexus, and Mercedes-Benz.) Even more than with leasing new cars, you want to make sure you do not get stuck paying the cost of major repairs. That could wipe out most of the savings you get with the lower payments on leasing versus buying.

CHAPTER 11

Scoping out Service: Finding the Right Dealer to Work on Your Car

Should you be worrying about future repairs, maintenance, and other service when you are still in the process of shopping for a new car or truck? Yes, but don't let it dominate your decision about which dealer to buy or lease from.

If you plan to bargain hard for the best price yourself or you are using a buying service or Car Bargains to scout out the best available price, buy where you get the best deal even if it is too far from home for regular service visits.

Most auto manufacturers require all their dealers to do warranty work on any vehicle of their brand, no matter where it was bought. And dealers' reluctance in the past to work on new cars they did not sell has mostly evaporated. For most dealers, repair work is more profitable than selling new cars. And that includes work paid for by the manufacturer on vehicles still under warranty, even though the profit margin may be lower than for work on older cars no longer covered by warranty.

Thus wise dealers are eager to build their service business even if they did not sell you the car. Wherever you buy the vehicle, you can still become a long-term service customer of a dealer near you.

An Exception, of Course

There is one exception to this rule of not worrying too much about the service department. It applies if you plan to shop at one-price dealers. Courteous, pleasant, and competent service while you are buying and while you own the vehicle are the lures the one-price dealer offers to make you consider paying a bit more than rock-bottom price. If you are considering no-dicker shopping, check out the reputation of the dealer's service department before you go. A ho-hum or poor service record raises questions about this dealer's commitment to the whole customer-coddling no-dicker philosophy. Try a different one-price dealer or switch to an alternative approach like a buying service.

Think Ahead

Although you will not be choosing the dealer to buy from based on the service department except for this one case, it makes sense to be scoping out service alternatives even while you are shopping, perhaps when you are arranging a test drive. Manufacturers want customers to be satisfied with their dealers so they will consider the same brand the next time they buy. Thus automakers survey car buyers to see how satisfied they are just after they bought the car as well as later when they go in for warranty repair work. Based on these responses, they set a consumer satisfaction index, or CSI, for each dealership. Though dealers typically will not discuss their CSI in detail with customers, they won't hesitate to boast if they have an especially good one. When you are at the dealership:

• **Look for plaques or certificates commemorating customer satisfaction awards.**

Of course, it is easy to put up meaningless plaques or certificates that sound impressive. And some "Outstanding Dealer" awards are tied to the volume of new cars sold. But look for awards with the manufacturer's logo on them that specifically mention customer satisfaction.

• **Stop by the service department and look for consumer satisfaction plaques on the wall here, too.**

While you are at the service department, if you see customers leaving or picking up their cars, ask them how they are being treated. If someone is angry, he or she won't hesitate to tell you about it.

Get the Word

Don't underestimate word of mouth when it comes to sizing up dealer service departments. While you are still shopping for your new car or truck, start asking friends, neighbors, and the people you work with what they hear about good and bad dealers in your area for the nameplates that interest you. Word spreads fast, especially if someone feels angry or ripped off. A customer survey by Ford Motor Co. showed that someone who felt he or she had a good experience with a dealer service department told an average of four people about it. But those with bad experiences could not wait to tell their horror stories to an average of 11 people. If you see a car at the mall or elsewhere with a license plate holder from a dealer that interests you, hail the owner and ask about the service department there. Does he or she go there for service, and how satisfactory is it? Most people are happy to fill you in on their experience.

If you want to go one step beyond word of mouth, check your local Better Business Bureau or state attorney general's office to see if there are complaints on file against a dealer's service department. Most customers have to feel really badly served to go to the trouble of filing such a complaint. More than a handful of complaints can signal a problem.

Auto Club Ratings

If you are a member of the local affiliate of the American Automobile Association (and sometimes even if you are not), you can get a list of approved auto repair shops, including new-car dealerships. AAA has done the research for you, surveying recent customers of shops and checking local consumer agencies for any high volume of complaints. The result is a list of about 4,500 auto shops in 31 states, including most major cities. To be certified by the local auto club program, a service department must be equipped to do all kinds of automotive repair work. And it must have certified mechanics in any specialty where it offers service.

Certification comes from the National Institute for Automotive Service Excellence, which administers tests in eight different areas of automotive service (engine work, brakes, heating, and air-conditioning, for example). Nearly 400,000 mechanics nationwide now have such ASE certification, as it is called.

Members can get a list of AAA-approved service departments by calling their local auto club office. When you call your auto club, emphasize that you are interested in new-car dealers of certain makes that can do new-car warranty work, since the AAA-approved list includes independent repair shops as well. If you are a AAA member who went to a AAA-approved service department, your local auto club will step in and try to mediate if you have a continuing dispute with the dealership service department. If agreement still is not reached, the AAA will arbitrate the case. If it decides in your favor, the dealership is bound by the AAA agreement to accept the decision. If the decision is in the dealer's favor, you would still be free to take the complaint to a local consumer agency, small claims court, or any other available forum. (Some local clubs will give the recommendations to nonmembers as well, a national AAA spokesman says, but only members get complaint resolution and other affiliated services.)

Watch Those Certifications

Even if you do not go through the AAA, the ASE certifications that the AAA uses to screen service departments still can be useful for you. Some dealerships will have ASE certificates of individual mechanics on the wall in the customer waiting area. But do not assume that one or two of these certificates mean that all work will be done by a certified mechanic. "The certification may be for working on brakes," says an official of the institute that issues the certification. "That does not tell you anything about the quality of the work if you are there to have your air-conditioning repaired." When you are actually taking in a vehicle for warranty work, ask the service manager specifically if your repair will be done by an ASE-certified technician.

As you try to scope out service talking to friends and co-workers or checking out service departments otherwise, it helps to have a notion of how a service department should perform. Manufacturers say that dealerships that habitually rank high in customer satisfaction deliver in the following areas:

- If you call up needing repairs or other service, you get a scheduled service slot within 24 hours.
- When you take in your car, you never wait more than a few minutes for the service manager or an assistant to talk to you and write up the problem on your car.
- Most of all, the service department fixes your problem correctly the first time without having to take your car or truck back again.

Look for the Ride

One of the most annoying aspects of auto repair is dropping off your vehicle and then having to find a way to get home, to the office, or wherever you need to be. The best service departments typically make arrangements to drive you to your next stop, to loan you a car while yours is in the shop, and, in a few cases, to pick up your vehicle from your house and bring it back when it is fixed. Check for such arrangements when you are looking at service departments. Giving you a ride is certainly no proof that the mechanical work will be the best. But it does show that the dealership cares about its customers' convenience. And when it comes to auto service, that is a big plus.

Ranking Service by Brand

Once you have decided which car, truck, or van you want to buy, your next concern should be choosing among individual dealers for their service. But early in your selection process, you might consider which brands get the highest satisfaction ratings overall for reliability and for dealers' handling of customers. Each year the research firm J. D. Power and Associates surveys more than 30,000 car and truck buyers chosen at random after they have owned their vehicle for just over a year. The survey measures how trouble-free the owners thought their vehicles were and how they ranked their experience at the dealership when they went in for maintenance or repair work. The findings in the most recent report revealed this information:

• Despite U.S. gains in quality and customer satisfaction, cars with Asian and European nameplates on average matched one another and outpaced domestic brands.

• Japanese luxury cars **Lexus** and **Infiniti** retained their perennial spot atop the customer satisfaction list.

• **Saturn** finished third, one of only two domestic brands in the top ten. **Cadillac,** at seventh, is the other.

• The rest of the top 10, in order, are **Acura, Volvo, Audi, Honda, Mercedes-Benz,** and **Toyota.**

• The only other brands to finish above the industry average for cars were **Buick, Lincoln, Subaru, Mercury, BMW,** and **Nissan.**

Among the industry category of light trucks—which includes vans and sport utilities as well as pickups—**Toyota, Oldsmobile, Ford, Mazda, Nissan,** and **Mitsubishi** topped the list.

CHAPTER 12

Getting Down to the Deal: How to Negotiate with Confidence and Get the Best Price

So you have decided to compete for yourself and go for the gold—the best price available out there. But unlike an Olympian—or, for that matter, the car salesman—you have not practiced this event over and over. So you naturally feel anxious. And you have to play on your opponent's court—the dealership is where they keep the cars. But you can calm your anxiety, reverse many of the car salesman's advantages, and make sure he or she needs the sale much more than you need to take the deal being offered. This chapter will show you how to keep control of your emotions and the negotiations by

- Making sure that you are thoroughly prepared for the negotiation.
- Knowing what maneuvers to expect from the car salesman and his managers and how to react to each one.

Just as if you had to make an important presentation to your boss or a difficult client, have in mind what you will say in various circumstances. Don't go to negotiate with your old gardening clothes still on. You don't have to put on your office gear (unless you are stopping straight from the office), but try to look reasonably prosperous.

CHECKLIST

Before you leave home, did you

1. Find out the dealer's invoice price of the car, truck, or van you are shopping for?_____

2. Find out if consumer rebates or dealer incentives are available so you can factor them into your target price?_____

3. Develop an educated guess at how badly the dealer needs to sell this vehicle, based on whether it is in limited supply (such as hot four-wheel drives or new sporty models) or selling slowly (indicated by incentives or splashy ads pushing that model in the auto section)?_____

4. Set your ultimate target price and decide where you will start bidding?_____ (For a full discussion of setting your target price, see Chapter 6.)

Remember, you will start the bidding as low as you reasonably can, but not so low that you will seem like an uninformed buyer just making a lowball offer.

Pull together a folder showing your data and sources on these details where you can readily refer to them yourself or show them to the salesman.

Let the Games Begin

When you get to the dealership, a salesperson likely will approach you. Establish quickly that you are a serious buyer, not a browser. If you come across as just shopping, the salesman (or woman) will be eager to move on to a likelier sale.

BE SPECIFIC

This establishes that you have done your homework. Don't say, "I'm looking at the Ford Taurus." Say instead, "I plan to buy a Ford Taurus LX within the next two weeks, and I know pretty much how I want it equipped. I will buy where I get the best price. Let's talk about it."

That keeps you in control. The salesman wants to know as much about you as possible to start spotting potential profit points. He may ask, "Do you have a trade-in?" or, "Will you be financing with the dealership?" Be polite but noncommittal, with something like "We can talk about that, but let's talk price first." Turn away even seemingly innocuous questions, such as "What do you do?" These are part of the salesman's "qualifying" process to make sure you are a serious, creditworthy buyer. And if you already have arranged a bank or credit union loan, you won't need to worry about that. Stay pleasant, but just say, "We can talk about me later. Let's talk about the Taurus price."

ESTABLISH WHAT THE PRICES INCLUDE

The salesman will try to focus on the MSRP or list price for the car and make it sound as though you are getting a big discount. You want to be sure you know what price you are hearing. He may say, "Well, we have a white Taurus with a remote entry system and a CD player, which you want. Because of this sale we are having, we can knock $800 off that and get you in this car for just $21,635."

You say, "Is that before the transportation charge and dealer advertising fee?" You cannot avoid these charges. In 1996 the transportation charge nationwide for a Taurus would have been $500. The advertising fee for regional ads for all dealers of that make varies locally. In Denver, for example, it would have been $91 in 1996. The salesman is likely to try to quote as low a figure as possible, but with those other charges, his quoted price becomes $22,226. And state sales tax and license plate fees will always be add-ons.

BRING UP THE INVOICE PRICE

You want to switch the discussion away from discount from list price and over to how much you intend to bid over the dealer's invoice cost. Bring out your price guide, World Wide Web printout, or mailing from a custom service like Intellichoice or Fighting Chance to show you have done your research on this.

Having done your homework, you know that the 1996 base invoice price for this Taurus LX is $19,137. For the package you want to add that includes an automatic brake system, an alarm, and remote unlocking system, the invoice price is $766. And the invoice on the CD changer that will make that drive to work a pleasure is $530. So the total invoice price is $20,433. With transportation and ad fees that becomes $21,024. Since a manufacturer's consumer rebate and recent newspaper stories have let you know that the Taurus is selling slowly, you have set your target price at no more than about 1%, or $200, over the invoice price.

STAND YOUR GROUND

The salesman is likely to say, "That is not the right invoice price for the car." He or she may in fact know less than you do, since traditional dealer training focuses on the MSRP and many dealers do not give salesmen the invoice prices.

Say, "This is the invoice price for the car I want with the equipment I want." Show him your price guide or printout.

START LOW

Though your target is $200 above invoice, you need to leave room for the dealership to budge you a little. So start out bidding at the invoice price on a car like the Taurus that is selling slowly. You know you are entitled to the $600 consumer rebate, but you do not bring that up yet. If that $600 had been a dealer instead of consumer sales incentive payment, you would start out bidding to try to capture at least half that money. In that case you would bid $500 below invoice and make it clear how you got that figure. "Since the dealership stands to get a $600 payment from Ford as a sales incentive, $500 below invoice seems fair."

PARRY THE PITY MOVE

The salesman may say something like "We've got families to feed, too. How can we make a profit when you are bidding just our invoice cost?" Having done your homework, you know that Ford pays a 3% holdback to dealers—or $673 on the $22,435 MSRP before transportation and advertising fees. So you say, "You will be making almost $675 on the holdback." He may try to dispute this, too, but stand firm again.

DON'T PLAY THE WAITING GAME

At this point the salesman is likely to say something like "I think this is way too low, but I will take your offer to my sales manager and see what I can do for you." He or she may not even intend to talk to the sales manager yet but plans to keep you waiting in the glassed-in office to pressure you into a higher offer before even seeking approval. Tell him or her you do not intend to wait long. Then don't just sit there. "I never just stay in the closing room," says Eric Skopec, coauthor of *Everything's Negotiable . . . When You Know How to Play the Game* and a veteran car buyer. "I wander around the showroom floor and check out other cars. That usually brings the salesman back quickly." You can be sure he will bring the news that your initial offer was not good enough. At this point, if you started the bidding at the invoice price, agree to $100 over invoice. (Remember, invoice plus $200 is your target.)

After a round of this, the salesman may bring back his sales manager or other superior, who will again say he cannot possibly make a profit at your bid. Repeat that you know about the $675 from the holdback. Let's say at this point the sales manager switches tactics and talks in terms of an amount over the invoice. You have won a victory—the discussion has shifted to your terms. But the sales manager says his lowest possible bid is $500 over invoice. Thank him and tell him you will consider his offer along with the others you have. Get his business card and get ready to leave. But before you go, double-check the invoice price involved and exactly which vehicle you are discussing.

WATCH THE EQUIPMENT

When you are planning to buy a car from the dealer's inventory, you are unlikely to find one on his lot equipped precisely in your dream package. (To get a car exactly as you want it, consider a factory order. See Chapter 8.) So if he has one in a color you would not mind in your driveway, you may have to be flexible. But be careful. Don't let the dealership bump you up to a much-better-equipped vehicle and blow right past your budget.

For instance, on the Taurus we have been discussing, the salesman might say: "The Taurus we are talking about has the luxury package with a super sound system. It will fit in well with your CD player." From your printout you can identify this package that also includes air-conditioning with electronic controls and chrome wheels and see that it adds $938 to the invoice price and $1,055 to the list price. Those are budget-busting numbers. So say, "No, I have to stick to my budget, and those options put me over."

If you catch the right dealer on the right day, you might wind up getting a better-equipped car for your original price. A colleague of mine went in to bargain on a Ford Explorer with a budget firmly in mind. The dealer wanted to move a particular Explorer on the lot. "I don't want a moonroof or leather seats," she kept saying when they were trying to get her to split the difference on the cost. "So I don't see any reason to pay for them." They wound up selling her the luxury model at her original bid for a lower-priced one.

ASK ABOUT A DEALER SWAP

Ask the salesman, "If we could agree on a price, is there a chance you could get this model from another dealer?" Computerized regional inventory lets each dealer spot what his fellow Ford, Chevrolet, Toyota, or other brand dealers have on their lots. He may be able to make a deal to swap for what you want with a dealer who is farther away than you want to travel to shop or who might not be willing to sell to you at as low a price. Meanwhile that dealer may have a buyer for the more luxuriously equipped Taurus you do not want.

But before the salesman checks to see if a swap might be possible, make sure it will not add to your cost. Many dealers that bid through Car Bargains offer the same price if the car can be located from another dealer within 50 miles or so. Don't pay more than $50 extra for such a swap unless you already are pretty sure from shopping that you cannot find the car you want at local dealers. (Don't admit you know that, even though the dealer can tell it from his computer check.) In that case you might agree to an extra $100 for the swap if you are not exceeding your budget.

REMEMBER, YOU CAN ALWAYS LEAVE

Don't get caught up in the game and spend all morning at one dealership when you planned to spend an hour at most. Remember, the dealer needs to sell that Taurus today, but you can always come back another day or go to another dealer. That gives you the leverage in this bargaining. If the process is moving too slowly, give the salesman your phone number and tell him or her, "You know the price I am looking for. Call me if your sales manager says he can meet it."

"If you leave, that puts the pressure on the salesman. He has to make the next move if he wants your business," counsels negotiations specialist Eric Skopec. Repeat that you intend to buy soon (you don't want to be written off as just a shopper, not a buyer). But mention again that you are shopping other dealers as well. Dealers who know they are competing with others are much likelier to consider lowering prices.

KEEP THE COMPETITION GOING

Unless you scored right away and closed a deal for your target price on your first day's visiting, play the offers you have so far against one another. Let's say, for instance, your lowest offer to date is $300 over invoice price—or $21,324 for the Taurus we have been discussing. Call back the same salesman you met with. Tell him you still intend to buy a car soon, remind him of the previous bid. Tell him it is still more than you can pay, but that a slightly better price might change your mind—but be noncommittal about exactly how much. You do not want to seem to commit to buy at a certain price. Let's say he calls back and offers $21,224—hitting your target of $200 over invoice price. Remind him that you have a $600 rebate coming from Ford on the car, effectively lowering your price to $20,624 plus sales tax and license fees. But do not jump at the deal. Politely tell him you will call him back within 48 hours or so.

Then call back the dealership that last offered $500 over invoice. Get the sales manager if you can. If not, talk to the salesman again. Say (if it's true) that you would like to buy from his dealership because it is more convenient to your home or office but that you have a bid of $21,224 before the consumer rebate and you will stick with that unless he can beat it. He may refuse to match the deal; if so, you still can take your last bid. He may bid $50 below the $21,224. Or he may just match it. In these last two cases, tell him you will get back to him shortly and call back the competing dealer. If that dealer really needs your transaction to meet a Taurus sales target for the month, he might drop to $100 above invoice. You have beaten your target price with your persistence. Unfortunately your work is not yet done.

Trade-in Time

Only after a new-car price is fully agreed upon should you even consider talking about trading your old car or dealer financing. If you have done your homework, you will have alternatives to both. You will know what your car is worth from checking local ads and visiting used-car departments of dealers who handle your make of car. (See Chapter 5 for details.) But, especially if your car is a popular model in good condition and you are sticking with the same brand, you might match or slightly beat that price with your new-car dealer, who sees potential profit in selling your used car. But do not expect an inflated trade-in value; the price of your new vehicle already is set, and that is the way you wanted it. If the trade-in offer is a good one, say yes. If not, take it back to the dealer where you got the best bid or write an ad to sell it.

Your price is set, but you still have to make sure you do not give back any of the good deal you have worked so hard for, as we will see in the next chapter.

Dealer No-Nos

If you followed this strategy, you are well on your way to a good deal. But be sure to avoid these cardinal sins of smart car negotiators. Any one of them can take you away from the focus you need to cut your best deal.

1. Never start out talking about monthly payments. This will tip the salesman off to your weak spot and let him dazzle you with the math involved in the financing. Focus on new car price.

2. Never start talking about your trade-in. Some buyers are in love with their old cars and care most about what they get for it. Trade-in comes later, if at all.

3. Never give them your car keys. Though this kind of abuse is fast disappearing, a few old-style salesmen will try to get your keys supposedly to check your trade and then try not to give them back until you sign a deal. Hostage taking is illegal, but do not give them a chance at it.

4. Do not write a deposit check until and unless a price is fully agreed upon and a contract signed. A "good faith" deposit while the sales manager is still considering your offer can make you a hostage just like the keys.

5. Do not talk about dealer financing until the price is fully agreed upon. Then have in mind the details of your loan from a local bank or credit union for careful comparison.

CHAPTER 13

Closing the Deal: Making Sure You Don't Sign away the Savings You Just Negotiated

Your salesman or the sales manager will refer to it as "doing the paperwork" or "putting your deal into the computer." But the finance manager you are about to meet aims to add profit for the dealership in your transaction without your even noticing it. He or she will offer tantalizing mechanical and financial add-ons and, if you are financing through the dealership, play with your monthly payments to make it sound as though you are not paying much more for those extras. You keep things simpler—and make yourself much harder to manipulate—if you already have arranged financing from an outside bank or credit union. (See Chapter 7.) But you may want to check to see if the dealer is offering cheaper financing.

CLOSING CHECKLIST

Before you meet the finance closer (in a separate visit to the dealership if you have agreed on the selling price in a telephone follow-up), make sure you have done the following:

1. Checked to see if the manufacturer is offering any special financing deal.____

The Taurus in our example earlier carried an offer of financing with 2.8% annual percentage rate at a time when the average loan rate was nearly 9%. But these deals can sound better than they are. Often the lowest rate applies to no more than a two-year loan when you were planning on a three- or four-year payment schedule. And the low rate typically is an either/or choice with the rebate being offered.

2. Figured the monthly payments on your outside financing once you know the price of the car.____

If you simply know that your rate is 8.5% from your bank, say, the dealership could be offering an 8% loan, but the finance manager is building in profit extras that boost the payments, you may not notice unless you know what the payments should be. (Use the worksheet and the table in Chapter 6 to figure your payments. Or your bank or credit union loan officer should be able to look it up for you.)

3. Checked the manufacturer's warranty on the vehicle so you are prepared when the finance closer inevitably asks you if you want to buy an extended warranty. ____

Detroit's Big Three recently were offering 36-month or 36,000-mile (whichever comes first) warranties with some luxury cars sporting longer terms.

In addition to dealer financing, the finance closer will be sure to pitch you on an extended warranty and credit life insurance. He will bring up items that are sold or installed by the dealer from independent suppliers—not the manufacturers. These can range from unneeded rustproofing and so-called fabric guard to possibly useful burglar alarms if the price is right.

Here is a rundown on what you will be offered as you are signing a supposedly finished deal and why, with a few possible exceptions, you want to just say no.

EXTENDED WARRANTY

If you are almost sure you will keep your car for five years or more, you might consider an extended warranty contract. But remember, your new-car warranty will cover your first three years. So check carefully into how the extended-warranty coverage kicks in and what it covers. (So-called power train–only warranties, for instance, may exclude expensive electronic repairs common in today's cars.) And an extended warranty can add from $400 to $1200 to the amount you are financing.

So if you think you are likely to switch cars again within four years or less, extended warranties make little sense. Research by the parent group of the car-pricing service Car Bargains estimates that the typical buyer might pay $800 for an extended warranty and collect only $300 in claims.

CREDIT LIFE INSURANCE

It sounds enticing. If anything happens to you, your spouse won't have to worry, the car loan will be paid off. The concept is good, but you will pay a lot more for protection at the car dealer than you will from your regular insurance agent. If you feel that you need such coverage, term life insurance or disability insurance is likely a much cheaper way to get it, and it will cover not only your car loan, but your mortgage and other debts as well.

If you are taking dealer financing (or, for that matter, signing a finance contract with the bank), be careful that insurance cost isn't just slipped in while you barely notice: "Just initial here so your family will be protected if, God forbid, anything happened to you," the finance manager might say.

FABRIC PROTECTOR

This is just another profit-building add-on. If your small kids tend to spill milk and juice in the backseat or the dog is likely to jump in with muddy paws, you can protect the fabric yourself with spray you can buy at your local discount store for $5 or so per can.

RUSTPROOFING

Once upon a time when cars were made of steel, a case could be made for rustproofing a new car in northern climates, where it would be assaulted by rain, snow, and salt over a long life. Now cars are made mostly of aluminum and plastic and are built by the manufacturer to resist rust for at least six to seven years. Manufacturers are so confident of this process that they provide anticorrosion warranties on new cars, usually covering the first 100,000 miles.

Thus nowadays dealer-sold rustproofing, which can cost you from $100 to $500, is nothing more than a way to add dealer profits. Even worse, some manufacturers—including General Motors, Toyota, and Volkswagen—warn that adding dealer rustproofing may invalidate the manufacturer's anticorrosion warranty.

When offered rustproofing, follow the example of the stolid Minnesota burghers in the movie *Fargo,* who turned down this option no matter how many times the hapless car sales manager pushed it on them. In fact, unless you decide you need an extended warranty, that is a good overall model for dealing with the finance manager: few words, most of them "No."

CHAPTER 14

Buying a Used Car: Getting the Most Car for the Least

The average new car costs nearly $18,500. The average used car costs about $11,000. For lots of good reasons, consumers are buying more used cars than ever (recently about 16 million used cars were sold in the United States annually, or one million more than new cars). But that growing urge to buy used boils down most of all to the math. This chapter will show you where to go—whether a new-car dealer, used-car superstore, or individual seller—to find the best trade-off among price, reliability, and convenience on used cars. And it will tell you what questions to ask when you get there.

In a thrift shop society that loves to get a good deal on everything from other people's antiques to used evening dresses, your neighbors aren't likely to think less of you for buying a smart-looking used car. More likely they will admire the deal you got. And the growing share of new cars being leased—recently about one-third—assures a steady stream of two- to four-year-old cars and trucks in relatively good condition—with safety features such as air bags and antilock brakes—that are turned in at the end of leases and usually then sold as used cars.

As consumers have demanded it, U.S. and foreign automakers have increased the reliability of their new cars—the eventual supply of used cars. The latest J. D. Power survey of owners of four- to five-year-old vehicles showed that truck owners had 11% fewer problems than in the previous year's survey and car owners 8% fewer—the fourth consecutive annual improvement for cars. And used-car loans—which once charged interest rates as much as two percentage points higher than new-car loans— now are not as expensive, at an average of about one percentage point over new-car rates.

ARE YOU A USED-CAR BUYER?

Despite the good deals available, not everyone is happy buying a used car. Answering the following questions will help you to see if you like the picture of yourself behind the wheel of a two- or three-year-old car:

1. Do you need a better car but resent paying—or quite simply cannot afford—new-car prices? Yes_____ No_____

(If you answered "Yes" here, you probably are among the majority of Americans. Since the mid-1980s new-car prices have risen more than 70%, while the overall measure of inflation, the Consumer Price Index, is up just about 40%.)

2. Rather than buying a new car, would you prefer to spend the $9,000 or so you would save buying an average used car on a new kitchen or a new computer system? Yes_____ No_____

(A "Yes" answer puts you in the majority again. In the most recent survey by CNW Marketing/Research in Bandon, Oregon, of what large purchases consumers most want to make, buying a new car was only number 11, while kitchen remodeling and new computers topped the list.)

3. If you bought a used car, would you invest some or all of the savings versus a new car to build up funds for retirement, college costs, or other future expenses? Yes_____ No_____

(Financial planner and author Jonathan Pond has calculated that in addition to the lower price itself, buying a used car can save you $5,300 over three years in lower sales tax, insurance and financing charges.)

4. Have you wished in the past for a better, more prestigious car—perhaps a luxury car—but felt you could not afford it? Yes_____ No_____

(Some luxury cars are good used-car buys because their price falls sharply from the new-car price after two or three years. And buying such a car used, you usually escape the so-called luxury tax—10% of any amount by which the car's purchase price that exceeds $32,000. That is, on a $38,000 car or sport utility, you would pay 10% of $6,000, or $600.)

Three or more "Yes" answers to these questions means you almost certainly should consider buying a good used car.

And the issue is not entirely financial. With the right buy you may get more emotional satisfaction from an upscale or sporty used car than a new one. A friend of mine had a failing old car and, wanting to get cheap and reliable transportation, intended to buy a new Plymouth Neon Sport, then priced at about $13,000, as he wanted it equipped. But he heard from a friend about a 1984 Mercedes-Benz 190 with just 58,000 miles, less than half the average mileage for a car that age, and no scratches or dents, selling for $6,500. He knew repairs lay ahead and fully expected to spend $2,000–$4,000 on mechanics' bills in the next few years. So he figured he would still wind up ahead financially. Now he enjoys the smoother ride from a heavy car (about 3,000 pounds vs. 2,400 for the Neon) and the comfortable leather seats. Best of all, he gets a great kick from owning a Mercedes.

The Opposition Case

Some considerations do override the savings on a used car for some people. A "Yes" answer to one of the questions below means you might not be happy buying a used car.

1. Does your age or regular long drives in isolated areas make the possibility of breakdown a major worry for you? Yes_____ No_____

2. Do you typically keep a car eight years or more before looking for a different one? Yes_____ No_____
(Though used cars today are more reliable than ever before, their previous use simply makes a breakdown or at least major repairs more likely than with a new car.)

Out of the Swamp

Once the piranha pool of what most Americans saw as a disgusting auto industry swamp (an annual Gallup poll on how much Americans respect various professions has never failed to place car salesmen last), used-cars sales methods are changing swiftly. At used-car superstores such as the CarMax chain started by electronics retailer Circuit City, you can look over an inventory of up to 800 used cars, go inspect the ones you like, and buy one with no haggling. At Saturn, Nissan, Lexus, or Mercedes-Benz dealers you can look over used cars inspected and reconditioned according to standards set by the manufacturers and carrying one- to three-year warranties. And at least some of Detroit's Big Three are expected to join this trend to manufacturer-sponsored used-car warranties.

Not Nirvana Yet

No, we are not about to tell you to relax and believe everything a used-car salesman tells you. Old habits die hard. The state attorney general of Connecticut charged recently that 40% of the used cars sold in the state had had their odometers changed to lower their mileage and make them look more attractive. (The local auto dealers association disputed this number, of course.) In California, state regulators have penalized Chrysler for sending to dealers as used cars vehicles that previously were turned back as lemons with mechanical defects. Chrysler denies the charges. (For more on dealing with lemon vehicles, see Chapter 15.)

Choosing a Used One

To decide what used vehicle you want to buy, follow the same process as for a new car—with one important addition. If you are interested in a particular make and model, you need to check closely on its record of reliability. First, to determine if you are looking for a large or small sedan, a pickup, van, or sport utility, you must ask these basic questions:

- How many people am I likely to be carrying?
- How much stuff do I haul?
- What is the primary purpose of this vehicle?

(For full details on choosing a vehicle—constructing your own auto-biography—see Chapter 2.)

Once you have decided what category you need (small sedan, sport utility, etc.), start checking recommendations for good used cars among such vehicles. In its annual April issue, **Consumer Reports** ranks virtually all cars, vans, and sport utilities on their value as used cars. Based on surveys of its readers, the magazine gives a detailed rundown of specific problems (engine, brakes, air-conditioning, etc.) experienced by versions of a particular model for the previous eight years, if it has been around that long. For instance, a 1991 Ford Tempo shows worse than average records in nine of 13 rated mechanical categories (with some data missing), average in four, and better than average in only one, body rust. Meanwhile a 1991 Honda Civic, a possible competitive choice, is better than average in 11 of 16 categories, average in three categories, and worse than average in only two. If it is not currently on the newsstand, the *Consumer Reports Annual Auto Issue* is available in most libraries, or write for back issues at $5 a piece to Back Issues Dept., Consumer Reports, P.O. Box 53016, Boulder, CO 80322-3016.

Always on the newsstand or in bookstores, *Edmund's Used Cars Prices and Ratings* ($6.95, updated quarterly) gives broader rankings for domestic and imported cars, vans, and sport utilities from the previous 10 years. The guide gives an overall ranking for each vehicle for each year, plus a breakout of rankings in six subcategories: safety, reliability, performance, comfort, fun to drive, and value. The first two are based on government statistics of safety tests and mechanical recalls. As the title suggests, this guide also gives prices.

Market research services also survey used-car owners. The J. D. Power survey on vehicle dependability, released annually in mid-March, is reported by many newspapers and magazines. You can find these articles through your library or periodical references from commercial on-line services.

Checking Prices

Once you have zeroed in on three or four choices that meet your needs and are rated as reliable used cars, start shopping for price. (If you need to be sure what you can afford, including sales tax and insurance, turn to the worksheet in Chapter 5.) Used cars give you more budget-adjusting options than new ones. If in mid-1996 a 1995 Audi 90 sounded too expensive at an average retail price of $20,025, dropping back a year to a 1994 model at $16,150 might be a lot more affordable for you.

As already mentioned, *Edmund's Used Cars Prices & Ratings* gives prices for used cars from the previous 10 years. It provides the original list price for a base model of the car at the start of each model year. Then you see the wholesale price (what you would be likely to get as a trade-in from a dealer if you owned that vehicle) and retail price (what a dealer is likely to charge if you go in to buy that car; prices from individuals selling their own cars may run roughly 10%–15% less). Remember, though, Edmund's prices are based on national averages; used-car prices can vary widely by region of the country depending on the popularity and supply of various models. The same data updated more frequently than the quarterly books is available on Edmund's World Wide Web site (http://www.edmunds.com).

The *NADA Official Used Car Guide,* a pocket-size orange book published by the National Auto Dealers Association, is one of the most widely used sources of used-car prices. It goes back for seven prior model years—three fewer than Edmund's guide. Look for the guide in your library or ask your insurance agent or bank or credit union loan officer to let you copy the pages you need. The version available on newsstands gives only the retail price, not the wholesale value, which you may need in your negotiating strategy.

The NADA guide publishes nine regionalized editions, so the prices you see there may well be closer to your hometown level than the national listings by Edmund's. But even more than with new cars, you are dealing in a local market. So check local classified ads for cars or trucks similar to those you are considering. If you prefer to use the phone, *Consumer Reports* will give you regionalized used-car prices for your area on a 900 telephone line (900-446-0500) at $1.75 a minute. If you wish, this help line will also give you the magazine's reliability ratings on specific used cars.

Setting Your Target Price

With this homework in hand, you can assess the prices at used-car superstores or other one-price dealers or set your negotiating strategy if you will be buying from a traditional dealer or an individual seller.

Here is a rundown of the places to shop for used cars. The fast-spreading used-car superstores are pushing the expansion of the Saturn-style one-price no-dicker approach for used cars. That concept is likely to spread faster for used cars than new ones simply because used cars are much harder for consumers to compare than used ones.

Superstores

Led by Circuit City's CarMax with 11 locations in southeastern states and plans to go national (with competing chains jostling to get started) these used-car megastores may eventually revolutionize how cars are sold. Circuit City says it plans to reach 80–90 stores within five years. For now, if you go to a CarMax location in suburban Atlanta, say, you can leave the kids in the lot's day care center while you concentrate on cars. Then you type into a computer terminal the price, make, and model car you are looking for. For cars that match your criteria, you get a picture on the computer monitor plus price and other details. If you are interested, you also get the location on the huge lot where the car is sitting among the 800 or so out there.

Cars are arranged by size type and price. Thus if, for example, you went out to see a 1994 Ford Explorer, you likely would find some Jeep Grand Cherokees, Nissan Pathfinders, and other sport utilities of similar vintage sitting near it. (Bring along your price guides in case you want to check out some of these as well.) CarMax will not discuss its pricing policies, but you will be able to approximate how much over trade-in value and how close to average retail value the no-dicker prices are.

If you are a haggle-averse shopper or even just a hurried one, you may well find the experience at CarMax (and its competitors, such as Car Choice in Dallas and AutoNation, just about to open its first outlets) much easier and less aggravating than any car shopping you have done in the past.

Drawbacks: You likely will not get the very best price at the superstores. If you can find a similar car on the used-car lot of a new-car dealer nearby (a '94 Explorer at a Ford dealer, for instance), you may well find a dealer who will bid $100 or more below the superstore price. But remember, you cannot assume—as you can with new cars—that the two vehicles are truly comparable.

Auto Malls

Predating corporate superstores, some 170 auto malls collect a variety of dealerships, sometimes with different owners, in one location so consumers can comparison shop two or more brands of new cars at once. And the trade-ins taken by all the new-car dealerships are typically pulled together in one lot to be sold as used cars. Thus, like the superstores, the auto malls enable you to look at multiple brands of used cars at once with a greater choice.

For example, the Mauro Auto Mall in Kenosha, Wisconsin, has 12 new-car franchises and on a given day has about 500 used cars from all those brands on the lot. By contrast, a typical independent dealer might have a maximum of 100 used cars concentrated in the one or two brands it sells new. The Mauro mall is one of a handful using a one-price selling system. But as competition from the superstores spreads, more used-car operations may well adopt it to compete for the no-haggle market. Saturn dealers, following their new-car policy, already have adopted one-priced selling for their used cars.

Executives of existing one-price malls say they aim to set their prices slightly below the average NADA guide prices for the same models. Haggle-ready used-car operations at malls are likely to boast prices competitive with one- or two-brand independent dealers because of cost savings from cooperative efforts in advertising and some other expenses.

Drawbacks: If you already are focused on one particular used vehicle rather than shopping several, you might find a bigger selection elsewhere. For instance, if you know you are looking for a high-volume used car such as the 1994 Ford Explorer previously mentioned, the largest Ford dealer in the area might have a bigger choice than a mall where Ford is just one of 10 or more brands sold.

Independent New-Car Dealers

Like the dealers in auto malls, independent Chevrolet, Ford, Toyota, Honda, or other dealers tend to get the best of the used-car flow both from their own trade-ins and from cars returning from leases that they originated. These cars may be new enough that the original manufacturer's warranty is still in effect and can be transferred to you as the next buyer. (For instance, a car returned after a two-year lease with 24,000 miles would still have a year or 12,000 miles left on a typical new-car warranty.) And with their own repair facilities, new-car dealers (like the superstores) are more likely than used-only dealers to repair problems they see on their used cars.

If it is a Saturn, Nissan, Infiniti, Lexus, Jaguar, Mercedes-Benz, or other brand that has a certified used-car program, a fresh-starting used-car warranty may cover one to three years even if the new-car warranty is expired. Even on brands without such warranties, the dealership itself will often write warranties that cover any defects you discover within the first 60 days you own the car.

Drawbacks: For more reliability and accountability, you pay higher prices. Used-car lots and especially individual sellers will be offering the same model and year used cars more cheaply.

Used-Car Dealers

The prices are lower, and used-car dealers may be conveniently located, but this story is mostly drawbacks.

Drawbacks: The cars they get may have been sent to auctions by dealers who did not want them. Used-only dealers are not as likely as new-car dealers to have effective warranties and to stand by them. And a practiced used-car salesman at one of these lots is much more likely than an individual seller to convince you that a car or truck is in better shape than it really is.

Individual Sellers

The main advantages to buying from an individual seller are price, price, and price. With no expenses comparable to those of dealers, they often are selling their used cars at prices 10%–15% below the average NADA price for dealers. This alternative works best if you or a friend are at least semiskilled at spotting potential mechanical problems. You can be almost sure that an individual ready to sell a car will not sink money into needed major repairs, and if you discover a defect after you bought it, you have no warranty. Possibly your only recourse against an unrepentant seller is small claims court or a similar time-consuming procedure.

Drawbacks: Buying this way will take more time tracking down cars from classified ads, talking to sellers on the phone, and traveling to look at likely candidates.

Getting Mechanical

Especially if you are seriously considering buying a used car from an independent used-car dealer or individual in "as is" condition with no warranty, get a mechanic of your choice to inspect the car. Expect to pay $75–$125 for this inspection, but consider it money well spent, possibly saving you from a costly error in buying the car.

An individual seller may understandably be reluctant to let you drive off alone to your mechanic in his or her vehicle. But often the logistics of this can be worked out if you seem a serious buyer.

Negotiating Price

If you are dealing with an individual seller or traditional dealer, tactics for negotiating your price are much the same as for new cars. Your ultimate weapon is to remain prepared to walk away from a car if you do not get the price you have determined to pay. But your advantage is not as clear as with a new car, where the salesman and you both know you likely can get another offer on almost exactly the same car down the road. With this in mind and because used cars are one of their biggest sources of profit, a dealer may not as readily slash his price on a used car to make the sale as he will on a new car. Still, you can negotiate. Some key points:

- Remember the NADA and other guide prices are just averages. A dealer may be asking and sticking to a slightly higher price for a car in especially good condition or with a manufacturer-backed warranty.
- Trade-in prices typically are 20% below the average retail price, the dealer's profit if he hits the average on a given car. Start bidding 5% over the trade-in price and aim to pay no more than average retail price if the car is in good condition. But be sure to check the adjustments for optional equipment or higher or lower than average mileage. Of course, you cannot know the dealer's specific trade-in price on that car, but using the average from a guide gives you a benchmark.
- Let's say in 1996 you were looking at a 1994 Dodge Neon Highline, which the dealer had priced at $11,100—near the average price for all used cars. You know from your price guide that the average retail selling price for this car is $10,875 and the average trade-in value is $9,000. Since the Neon you are looking at is in good but not perfect condition, you determine that your top price will be $10,700.
- To give yourself negotiating room, start your bid at $9,450—5% above the average trade-in. Give ground grad-

ually in one or two counteroffers, but when you reach $10,500 start to leave if your bid is not accepted. You might get lucky and have the salesman take you up on it. If not, make your final bid of $10,700, and if it is not accepted, actually do leave.

If you are not shopping at a dealer, your price guidelines change because neither an independent used-car dealer nor an individual seller is likely to have done the repair work needed on the car. Look for a price 10%–15% below the average dealer retail prices in the guides or on the World Wide Web.

Five Danger Signals

Used-car sellers often try to conceal high mileage and camouflage accident repair or rust damage. And of course you are looking for tip-offs to serious mechanical problems. Pass up a used car you are inspecting if you see any these warning signs:

1. Worn brake pedals don't seem to match the odometer reading. If a three-year-old car with 30,000 miles on the odometer has a badly worn brake pedal, it raises suspicions about the mileage.

2. An oil change sticker on the frame inside the car door shows a mileage and date that seems not to track with the odometer. Someone illegally turning back the odometer might forget about these stickers.

3. You see fluid leaks of black (oil) or red (transmission fluid) on the driveway or car lot where the car sits. If the seller can't even stop the leaks while showing the car, it may signal a serious engine or transmission problem.

4. You spot rust in the trunk, the panels under the doors, or the wheel wells. Rust on a car is like cockroaches in an apartment: one problem likely signals many more unseen ones.

5. You spot paint on wires or weather stripping in the trunk or the rubber seals in the gas cap openings. Ask for an explanation, but be skeptical. If the seller says it was just a minor accident, ask to see the receipt for the repairs.

The Depreciation Puzzle

When buying a new car, it pays to pick a model that holds its value well. Thus if you sell it within five years while it still holds substantial value, your loss from depreciation will be less than with other models. But when you are scouting for a good, affordable used car, the reverse is true. Cars that hold their value well will cost you more as used cars.

Models that are strong sellers as new cars tend to hold their value better. As the hottest category in recent years, for example, sport utilities almost all are expensive used cars. If you are determined to buy a used sport utility, let reliability be the tiebreaker.

To see how depreciation factors in, let's say that in 1996 you wanted to buy a three-year-old luxury sedan. A 1993 Mercedes 300E, which had a list price of $43,800 new, would cost $27,150—or 61% of its original value—as a used car, according to NADA figures. But a 1993 Lincoln Town Car Signature—with an above average mechanical record as a used car—has a better ratio. Listing for $35,494 new, it averages $17,100 as a used car, or 54% of its original list price. True, the Mercedes is a more expensive car all along. But that initial $8,306 gap over the Lincoln's original price widens three years later to $10,050. As a new car to be sold or traded in later, the Mercedes is a relatively better value. As a used car, the Lincoln is a better buy.

Crucial Questions

Wherever you plan to buy a used car—from a new or used car dealer or an individual—you want to start by asking the same questions. With individuals and some traditional car dealers that may have just one or two of the models you are interested in, you may be able to get most of these questions answered on the telephone—possibly ruling out a car even before you have made a trip to see it. Beyond the obvious details of model, year, optional equipment, and color, here are the crucial queries:

- How many owners has the car had?
- How long did the current or most recent owner keep it?
- Was most of the mileage put on in city driving or long highway trips (much easier on the vehicle)?
- Is there a comprehensive service and repair record?
- Why is the car being sold?
- Has the car been in any accidents?

A dealer may honestly not know the answers to some of these questions, and you cannot always be sure you are hearing the truth. But, for instance, if you learn that a service and repair record exists, you know you may have a better chance of measuring the true mechanical condition of the car and have a yardstick that may help you assess if the mileage on the odometer is correct.

CHAPTER 15

Got a Lemon? Don't Let It Squeeze You

Despite big gains by auto manufacturers in the last decade in turning out more reliable cars and trucks, rogue miscreant vehicles with one or more intractable mechanical problems still get sent to new-car dealerships. But your chances of buying a lemon are low. With used cars you can have a better chance of avoiding a mechanical nightmare if you do your homework and shun models with poor records as used cars. Nonetheless, you need to know your most effective remedies if you start to get a whiff of lemon.

For the really sour performers, all 50 states now have some form of "lemon law." Though they vary in detail, these laws hold out the potential of damages or a replacement vehicle in cases where a car or truck has been returned four times or more for the same repair or has been out of service for 30 days or more out of a specified period, often 12 months. Before getting to that stage, however, you will have to go through repeated repair attempts and complaints at lower levels. Keeping careful records is essential if you are to have any chance of success in your claim.

Preventitive Medicine

It will take a few months before you can be sure you are driving a lemon, and your dealings in the meantime (as well as solutions to lesser mechanical problems) will be smoother if you take your car to a dealership with a reputation for customer satisfaction with its service department. (For details, see Chapter 11.) Though new cars covered by a manufacturer's warranty can be taken for service to any dealer handling that brand, your options may be more limited if you buy a used car with a warranty. If your used-car warranty is issued by an individual dealer, you probably will have to have repair work done there. So before closing a used-car deal from a new-car dealership, check out its service reputation.

Chain of Complaint

No matter what its reputation, if you find a dealership has not solved your problem with its supposed repair, talk to the service manager (not just the person behind the desk who wrote up your invoice in the first place). Ask the manager to drive your car so he can see the transmission is still slipping, the engine is misfiring, or whatever. If the service manager still does not solve your problem, start laying a paper trail. Mail or fax a letter to the owner or general manager of the dealership. Play on his or her concern for the reputation of the business. Say (if true) that you had heard good reports about the dealership's service from your friends and you are surprised that your engine problem has not been fixed already.

On a new car covered by manufacturer's warranty, your next step, if the dealer still has not solved your problem, is the auto company's zone representative. The dealer can give you this number, or it may be listed in your new-car manual. Mail or fax a letter detailing your complaint in addition to your phone call. If the zone official still does not order the dealer to do the repair, move on to the owner relations department of the auto company—whose address and phone number definitely will be in your owner's manual. Your next step is to request arbitration under a program run by the manufacturer or contracted from an outside organization. This step likely will be stipulated in your warranty; check it to see what arbitration program it calls for. But before you agree to arbitration, be sure that you are not bound by the decision and that you can still take legal action if you wish. If it comes to that, you may be able to take the case to small claims court without paying to hire an attorney.

Lemon Action

If your frustration is mounting as you fail to get satisfaction from the dealer and manufacturer, consider filing under your state lemon law if your case meets the requirements. Check with the state attorney general's office for details. To set this procedure in motion, you usually have to send a certified mail notification, separate from your previous complaints, to the manufacturer that you are filing under the lemon law and requesting a replacement vehicle or reimbursement of your purchase price. The company and dealer usually then are given a final chance to repair the defect before the state will enforce the law. Some states, including populous ones such as Florida, Massachusetts, New Jersey, New York, Texas, and Washington, have state-run arbitration programs in connection with their lemon laws.

Used Cars and Exceptions

If you buy a used car carrying a warranty of 12 months or more, your state lemon law may cover it as well as new models. Check the attorney general's office to see if this is true. Even with a new car, exceptions to these laws can trip you up. Watch for these:

LEASING

Lemon laws in many states do not cover leased cars because the leasing company—not you, the driver—is the owner of record of that vehicle. If you are down to a close call between buying and leasing (see Chapter 4), the lemon law status of leased cars in your state might make a difference to your decision.

BROKER OWNERSHIP

Unlike the national auto-buying services discussed in Chapter 8, local car brokers sometimes take title to the cars they are buying before passing them along to their clients. In some states that can invalidate the lemon law coverage because the eventual owner was not the original owner. If you are considering a brokered purchase, check into this angle carefully before going ahead.

Beyond the Warranty

If your new-car or used-car warranty has expired, chances are so has your coverage under your state lemon law (although if you filed under the law before expiration and win your case, you could get coverage retroactively). Even if your repair problems start after your warranty has run out, however, you still have ways to complain and to get arbitration for your complaints.

Under the American Automobile Association program of approved repair shops, if you are a member of AAA and use an approved shop, the local auto club frequently will offer mediation, then arbitration, if you cannot settle a dispute with the shop. The decision is binding on the business, but not on you. If you lose arbitration, you still are free to take legal action or pursue other complaints. The local Better Business Bureau also may offer an arbitration program that you can use if you do not meet the requirements of the AAA arbitration. Beyond that, taking your complaint to a local consumer affairs office or a newspaper or broadcast "complaint hot line" sometimes can get results.

If all this sounds immensely time-consuming and frustrating, it is. So look up your state lemon laws, know your rights, and then hope you are among the majority of car owners who never have to exercise them.

CHAPTER 16

Down the Road: Mechanical Maintenance and Financial Planning

So you just got home with your new or slightly used car and probably are in the mood to go for a nice ride—not think ahead to your next car purchase a few years down the road. But as in all personal finance, planning well ahead is essential to meeting your goals. This chapter will show you how to be ready financially when it is time to buy or lease your next car.

Your first step is to read your owner's manual carefully and check out the recommended schedule of maintenance. Then tell yourself you are going to be dependable about sticking to that schedule. Careful, regular maintenance of your car or truck will make it worth more when you sell it or trade it in in a few years.

Regular oil changes are the most important maintenance chore, the one that can do the most to keep your engine in top shape. With improved engine technology, manufacturers have extended the recommended intervals between oil changes to as much as 7,500 miles. But mechanics counsel that if you want to be sure your engine stays healthy, change the oil and the oil filter at least every 5,000 miles. While you are being a model citizen and following the auto company's maintenance schedule, keep all your service receipts to prove that you did. Such receipts will add value to your vehicle when you get ready to sell or trade it.

Familiarize yourself with the warranty, including the fine print and the stipulations by the manufacturer on what might invalidate the warranty. Most repairs under the warranty must be done at an authorized dealer for your brand of car—but not necessarily the one where you bought the car. With some used-car warranties, however, you may be required to stick with the selling dealer for service. A typical new-car warranty includes "bumper-to-bumper" coverage for three years or 36,000 miles, whichever comes first. Some luxury brands, including Acura, BMW, Cadillac, Jaguar, Lexus, Mercedes, Saab, and Volvo, provide four-year/50,000-mile warranties. Some specialized components such as sound systems, batteries, and parts are not covered by the overall warranty but have specific and separate warranties of their own. These details ought to be spelled out in the package accompanying your owner's manual.

With car materials much more rust-resistant than they were in the past, most manufacturers give warranties against rusting through the vehicle body for as much as 100,000 miles. (Depending on the company, this coverage may or may not be transferable to used-car owners after the initial buyer.)

Automotive Financial Planning

Then you might start a savings account for your car (or, better yet, put money into a higher-interest money-market fund). Okay, you already are saving for the kids' college and your own retirement. But as we advised in Chapter 13, extended service contracts that cover you beyond the warranty period rarely are worth the price you pay for them. If you build up savings in an auto account, you are insuring yourself against postwarranty repair bills (and getting paid interest instead of paying inflated fees to an insurance company). In the happy event repairs don't use up your auto fund, you can apply what is left over toward your next new or used car.

In fact, financial planner Diahann Lassus of New Providence, New Jersey, counsels clients who have just bought a new car to start saving for the next one. If you expect to keep your car for six years, for example, and believe that a new car you want by that time is likely to cost $24,000, you would start putting aside $4,000 a year. Almost invariably, paying cash for a car is the cheapest way to buy it, and starting to save now might let you join the satisfied society of cash buyers. Of course, if other savings needs preclude a commitment that big, you are almost certain to find some good loan or lease deals when it comes time to get another car. And whatever you have saved can be used for a sizable down payment to reduce loan payments or even to cut lease payments.

Whenever that day will be, try to be sure you make it before your old car develops crippling problems that keep it out of service. A new- or used-car buyer who must have a car immediately is the least likely to get a good deal and the most likely to pay too much or be talked into options or add-ons he or she does not really need. Planning ahead means that when you shop you can always walk away from a car salesman's offer and look for a better one. And that keeps you where you want to be: on the road to another good deal.

CHAPTER 17

Summing up: Step by Step to a Great Deal

You now should be ready to find a great deal—on your own or with the help of a buying service. Just to be sure, go over this final checklist. Mostly "Yes" answers means you are a savvy shopper.

Before You Negotiate

Did you

1. Make decisions about buying or leasing, getting a new or used car, and whether to negotiate for yourself or hire someone to do it before you ever went near a car dealership?____

2. Go through a careful review of how many people and how much luggage or gear you normally handle in deciding if you need a minivan or just a minicommuter, a sport utility or a sedate sedan?____

3. Check the safety and theft records of various models not only to protect your family, but with the idea of saving money on your auto insurance?____

4. Look at possible candidates at the local auto show and arrange test drives at dealers, without negotiating, of the cars or trucks that interest you the most?____

5. Make a careful budget to see what vehicles you can afford, not forgetting to add in sales tax, insurance, and probable maintenance expenses?____

6. Make a careful assessment of what your old car is worth to trade in or sell, checking comparable vehicles in the classified ads and used-car price guides and possibly getting bids from used-car dealers?____

7. Check out the dealer's cost, using price guides or Internet Web sites, and watch for any rebates or other incentives?____

8. Set your target price using the "dealer invoice" price so you will know in advance what you intend to pay for your car or truck?____

9. Shop for a loan before you started shopping for a car, so you know that you have financing preapproved?____

Getting Down to the Deal

You have done your homework. Now remember

- If leasing interests you, analyze any possible deal carefully. Focus on total cost, not monthly payments. Negotiate the lease equivalent of selling cost, the "capitalized cost," to hit the same target price as if you were buying.

- When negotiating, stay focused on price. Do not be distracted by questions about a possible trade-in or dealer financing.
- State your opening bid. Make clear you know the invoice price and that you are bidding a certain amount above that. If there are dealer incentives from the manufacturer, spell out that you know that as well.
- Don't let a salesperson leave you stewing in a dealership office while he or she supposedly talks over your bid with the sales manager. Walk around the showroom floor, checking out other cars, and if your salesperson still does not return get ready to leave.
- If you are not making progress, go ahead and leave. The dealership needs this deal more than you do.
- Try to generate competing bids on the same car from different dealers. Such competition almost always produces the lowest possible price.
- Be as careful closing the deal as you were negotiating the price. Do not agree to an extended warranty or other costly add-on that could wipe out your savings.
- If you have decided on a used car, look for one that carries a warranty of a year or more, through the manufacturer.
- Though you are not likely to need it, be familiar with your state's "lemon law" that provides for damages or replacement vehicles in the case of real duds.
- If you have warranty or other repair complaints, keep careful records of invoices, letters, and faxes as you complain to higher and higher levels of the company or to local or state officials.
- You got your car or truck. Start planning for the next one.

GLOSSARY

Here is a rundown in alphabetical order of automotive terms you may encounter while shopping. Because leasing is a jargon-filled universe where mastering the terminology is essential, we have listed leasing terms under a separate heading.

Advertising fee. Dealers divide the cost of regional advertising. This add-on, often in the $100–$200 per vehicle range, unfortunately usually cannot be avoided by the buyer.

APR. Annual percentage rate—the true interest rate being paid on an auto loan, taking into account all fees and other charges.

Back-end options. Additional items the dealership will try to sell you after the price of your car has been set. This can include items like rustproofing, extended warranties, and credit life insurance. They will run up your bill—and the dealer's profits—unless you are wary.

Dealer swap. An exchange among dealers—usually within the same region—to get a customer a car or truck with the equipment he or she wants.

Freight. This charge for shipping the car to the dealer, recently running from $350 to $500, is added to any price agreed upon and rarely is negotiable. (Sometimes called **destination charges.**)

Holdback. An amount paid by the manufacturer to the dealer on each vehicle—usually 2%–3% of MSRP. The effect is to lower the dealer's cost below stated invoice price. Typically, a dealer will not negotiate a price low enough to cut into his holdback.

Invoice cost. The amount charged to a dealer by the manufacturer (and stated on the invoice) when a car is shipped to the showroom.

MSRP. Manufacturer's suggested retail price, the car's list price. You want to negotiate up from the invoice price, not down from the MSRP.

NADA Official Used Car Guide. Published by the National Auto Dealers Association, this orange pocket-size book gives wholesale and retail prices for used cars going back seven years.

Sticker price. Same as the MSRP. The list price stated on the window sticker.

Upside down. A car owner who has no equity in his vehicle. If he tried to trade in for a new car, he would have a negative trade-in—would owe the dealership money to pay off the old loan.

Leasing

Capitalized cost. The equivalent of the selling price in the lease transaction. In many cases you can negotiate this price just as you would if you were buying the car, resulting in lower monthly payments. The payments are determined by the difference between the capitalized cost and the residual value (see following).

Capitalized cost reduction. Jargon for down payment in a lease transaction. While the best lease deals usually involve no down payment, you can use it as a way to reduce the payments if, say, you have the proceeds from selling your old car.

Closed-end lease. A lease in which the residual value (the value at the end of the lease) is stated explicitly. With such a lease, the leasing company carries the risk that the vehicle might be worth less than the residual value. Never consider an open-end lease, where you bear that risk.

Depreciation. How much the car loses in value during the lease: the difference between the capitalized cost and residual value. The same term is used when you own the car—the difference between how much you paid for the new car and what your used car is worth at some point in the future.

Early termination. Ending a lease before its term is up. Early termination typically triggers penalties.

Excess mileage charge. A penalty for driving more than the allowance in your lease—usually 12,000–15,000 miles a year. Be careful that your lease contract has an allowance matching how much you are likely to drive.

Lessee. You, the consumer who leases the vehicle and must make the monthly payments.

Lessor. The company, usually a bank, finance company, or finance subsidiary of an auto company, that owns title to the car and leases it to you.

Purchase option. The right to buy the leased car or truck for a set price at the end of the lease. If you think you might consider buying, make sure your lease contains a purchase option.

Residual value. What the vehicle will be worth at the end of the lease. It may or may not match the best estimate of the market value of that used car after two, three, or four years. When a manufacturer wants to promote leasing of a certain model, it will lower payments by artificially boosting the residual value.

APPENDIX A

Insurance Costs: How Cars, Trucks, Vans, and Utilities Stack Up

When you are considering a new vehicle, the insurance bills you will pay for comprehensive and collision coverage are an important part of your budget. Based on their records of collision repairs and theft, some cars and trucks cost more to insure than others. Here is a rundown of rankings by Insurance Services Office of how vehicles compare with others in the same class.

Make and Model	Cost to Insure
SMALL CARS	
Chevrolet Beretta	High
Chevrolet Camaro	High
Chevrolet Cavalier	Average
Chevrolet Corsica	Average
Dodge Avenger	Average
Dodge Neon	Average
Dodge Stratus	Average
Eagle Summit	High
Eagle Talon	High
Ford Aspire	High

Make and Model	Cost to Insure
SMALL CARS	
Ford Contour	Average
Ford Escort	High
Ford Probe	High
Geo Metro 2-door hatch	V. High
Geo Metro 4-door	High
Geo Metro Lsi 2-door hatch	V. High
Geo Metro Lsi 4-door	High
Geo Prizm	Average
Honda Civic	High
Honda Civic DX 4-door	Average
Honda Civic LX 4-door	Average
Honda Prelude	High
Hyundai Accent	Average
Hyundai Sonata	High
Kia Sephia	Average
Mazda Protege	Average
Mercury Mystique	Average
Mercury Tracer	High
Mitsubishi Eclipse	High
Mitsubishi Galant	Average
Mitsubishi Mirage	High
Nissan 200SX	High
Nissan Sentra	High
Oldsmobile Achieva	Average
Oldsmobile Ciera	Low
Plymouth Neon	Average
Pontiac Grand Am	Average
Pontiac Sunfire	Average
Saturn SC	Average
Saturn SL	Average
Saturn SW	Average
Toyota Corolla	Average
Toyota Paseo	High
Toyota Tercel	High
Volkswagen Golf	Average
Volkswagen Jetta	Average

Make and Model   Cost to Insure

MIDSIZE CARS—UNDER $20,000

Make and Model	Cost to Insure
Acura Integra LS 2-door	High
Acura Integra LS 4-door	Average
Acura Integra RS 2-door	High
Acura Integra RS 4-door	Average
Buick Century	Low
Buick Regal	Low
Buick Skylark	Average
Chevrolet Camaro	High
Chevrolet Cavalier	Average
Chevrolet Lumina	Low
Chevrolet Monte Carlo	Average
Chrysler Cirrus	Average
Chrysler Concorde	Low
Chrysler Sebring	Average
Dodge Avenger	Average
Dodge Intrepid	Low
Dodge Stratus	Average
Eagle Summit	Average
Eagle Talon TSi	High
Eagle Vision	Low
Ford Contour	Average
Ford Mustang	V. High
Ford Probe	High
Ford Taurus	V. Low
Ford Thunderbird	Average
Honda Accord	Average
Honda Civic	Average
Honda Prelude	High
Hyundai Sonata	High
Mazda 626	High
Mazda MX-5 Miata	Average
Mercury Cougar XR7	Average
Mercury Mystique	Average
Mercury Sable	V. Low

Make and Model	Cost to Insure
MIDSIZE CARS—UNDER $20,000	
Mitsubishi Eclipse	High
Mitsubishi Galant	Average
Nissan 200SX	High
Nissan 240SX	High
Nissan Altima	Average
Nissan Sentra	High
Oldsmobile Achieva	Average
Oldsmobile Cutlass Supreme	Low
Pontiac Firebird	High
Pontiac Grand Am	Average
Pontiac Grand Prix	Low
Pontiac Sunfire	Average
Subaru Impreza	Average
Toyota Camry DX 2-door	Average
Toyota Camry DX 4-door	Low
Toyota Camry LE	Average
Toyota Celica	High
Toyota Corolla	Average
Volkswagen Cabriolet	High
Volkswagen GTI	High
Volkswagen Jetta	Average
Volkswagen Passat	Average
MIDSIZE CARS—OVER $20,000	
Acura Integra GS-R 2-door	High
Acura Integra GS-R 4-door	High
Buick LeSabre	Low
Buick Regal	Low
Chevrolet Caprice	Low
Chevrolet Impala	Low
Chrysler Sebring	Average
Dodge Intrepid	Low
Dodge Stealth	Average

Make and Model	Cost to Insure
MIDSIZE CARS—OVER $20,000	
Eagle Talon TSi	High
Eagle Vision	Low
Ford Crown Victoria	Low
Ford Mustang	V. High
Ford Taurus	V. Low
Honda Accord	Average
Infiniti	Average
Mazda 626ES	High
Mercury Grand Marquis	Low
Mercury Sable	V. Low
Mitsubishi Eclipse	High
Mitsubishi Galant	Average
Nissan 240 SX	High
Nissan Altima	Average
Nissan Maxima	Average
Oldsmobile Cutlass Supreme	Low
Oldsmobile 88	Low
Pontiac Bonneville	Low
Pontiac Firebird Trans Am	High
Saab 900	Average
Subaru Legacy	Average
Toyota Avalon	Average
Toyota Camry LE	Low
Toyota Camry LE V6 2-door	Average
Toyota Camry LE V6 4-door	Low
Toyota Camry SE V6 2-door	Average
Toyota Camry SE V6 4-door	Low
Toyota Camry XLE	Low
Toyota Celica GT convertible	High
Volkswagen Jetta GLX	Average
Volkswagen Passat	Average

Make and Model	Cost to Insure
LARGE CARS—UNDER $25,000	
Acura 2.5 TL	Average
Acura 3.2 TL	Average
Audi A4	Average
Audi A6	Low
BMW 328i	High
Buick LeSabre	Low
Buick Park Avenue	V. Low
Buick Riviera	Average
Buick Roadmaster	Low
Chrysler LHS	Low
Chrysler New Yorker	Low
Infiniti I30	Average
Lexus ES 300	Low
Mazda Millenia	Average
Mercedes-Benz C220	Average
Mitsubishi 3000 GT	Average
Nissan Maxima GlE	Average
Oldsmobile Aurora	Average
Oldsmobile LSS	Low
Oldsmobile 98 Regency Elite	V. Low
Pontiac Bonneville SSE	Low
Saab 900	Average
Saab 9000	Average
Toyota Avalon	Average
Volvo 850	Low
Volvo 960	Low

Make and Model	Cost to Insure
LARGE CARS—OVER $25,000	
Audi A6 Quattro	Low
Audi Cabriolet	Average
BMW 328i convertible	High
BMW 750 iL	Average
BMW 850 Ci	Average

Make and Model	Cost to Insure
LARGE CARS—OVER $25,000	
Cadillac DeVille	V. Low
Cadillac Eldorado	Low
Cadillac Fleetwood	Low
Cadillac Seville	V. Low
Chevrolet Corvette	Average
Infiniti J30	Average
Infiniti Q45	Average
Jaguar Vanden Plas	Average
Jaguar XJ6	Average
Jaguar XJ12	Average
Jaguar XJR	Average
Jaguar XJS	Average
Lexus GS 300	Average
Lexus LS 400	Low
Lincoln Continental	V. Low
Lincoln Mark VIII	Average
Lincoln Town Car	V. Low
Mazda Millenia	Average
Mercedes-Benz	Average
Mercedes-Benz C280	Average
Mercedes-Benz E300	Average
Merceds-Benz E320	Average
Mercedes-Benz S320	Average
Mercedes-Benz S420	Average
Mercedes-Benz S500	Average
Mercedes-Benz SL	Average
Saab 900 turbo convertible	Average
Saab 9000	Low
Subaru SVX LSi	Average
Volvo 960 wagon	Low
SPORT UTILITIES	
Acura SLX	Low
Chevrolet Blazer	Average
Chevrolet Suburban	Low

Make and Model	Cost to Insure
SPORT UTILITIES	
Chevrolet Tahoe	Average
Ford Bronco	Low
Ford Explorer	V. Low
Geo Tracker	High
GMC Jimmy	Average
GMC Suburban	Low
GMC Yukon	Average
Honda Passport	Average
Isuzu Trooper	Low
Jeep Cherokee	Average
Jeep Grand Cherokee	Average
Land Rover Discovery	Average
Land Rover Range Rover	Average
Mitsubishi Montero	High
Suzuki Sidekick	High
Toyota 4-Runner	High
Toyota Land Cruiser	High
MINIVANS	
Chevrolet Astro	Low
Chevrolet G30 Sportsvan	Average
Chevrolet Lumina	Low
Chrysler Town & Country	V. Low
Dodge Caravan	V. Low
Dodge Grand Caravan	V. Low
Ford Aerostar	Low
Ford Chateau Club Wagon	Low
Ford Club Wagon	Low
Ford Windstar	Average
GMC G3500 Rally Wagon	Average
GMC G3500 Vandura	Average
GMC Safari	Low
Honda Odyssey	Average

Make and Model	Cost to Insure
MINIVANS	
Mazda MPV	Average
Mercury Villager	Low
Nissan Quest	Low
Oldsmobile Silhouette	Low
Plymouth Grand Voyager	V. Low
Plymouth Voyager	V. Low
Pontiac Trans Sport	Low
Toyota Previa	Low
PICKUPS	
Chevrolet Fleetside	Average
Chevrolet Sportside	Average
Chevrolet S-10	Average
Dodge Dakota	Average
Dodge Ram	Average
Ford F150	Low
Ford F250	Low
Ford Ranger	Average
GMC Sierra	Average
GMC Sonoma	Average
Mazda B2300	Average
Mazda B3000	Average
Mazda B4000	Average
Mitsubishi Mighty Max	High
Toyota T100	Average
Toyota Tacoma	Average

APPENDIX B

Record of Injuries

The Highway Loss Data Institute keeps records of injuries reported as insurance claims in various models of cars, trucks, vans, and sport utilities. Here, in alphabetical order, are vehicles compared with their own size and type. The lower the number, the better the rating. The average for all vehicles equals 100.

Model	Injury
4-DOOR CARS	
Large	
Acura Legend	78
Buick LeSabre	53
Buick Park Avenue	54
Buick Roadmaster	56
Chevrolet Caprice	61
Chrysler Concorde	53
Chrysler New Yorker	65
Dodge Intrepid	70
Eagle Vision	75
Ford Crown Victoria	64

Model	Injury
4-DOOR CARS	
Large	
Mercury Grand Marquis	63
Oldsmobile Eighty-Eight	60
Oldsmobile Ninety-Eight	54
Pontiac Bonneville	63
Average	61
Midsize	
Buick Century	71
Buick Regal	69
Chevrolet Cavalier	117
Chevrolet Corsica	117
Chevrolet Lumina	81
Chrysler LeBaron	90
Dodge Spirit	103
Ford Taurus	82
Ford Tempo	123
Honda Accord	96
Honda Civic	119
Hyundai Sonata	183
Infiniti Q20	105
Lexus ES 300	74
Mazda 626	106
Mercury Sable	80
Mercury Topaz	120
Mitsubishi Diamante	84
Mitsubishi Galant	119
Nissan Altima	125
Nissan Maxima	110
Oldsmobile Cutlass Sierra	70
Oldsmobile Cutlass Supreme	57
Plymouth Acclaim	105
Pontiac Grand Prix	69
Pontiac Grand Am	104

Model	Injury
4–DOOR CARS	
Midsize	
Pontiac Sunbird	131
Saturn SC	96
Subaru Legacy	117
Subaru Legacy 4WD	92
Toyota Camry	95
Volkswagen Passat	110
Volvo 850	63
Average	98
Small	
Dodge Shadow	147
Ford Escort	118
Geo Metro	152
Geo Prizm	127
Hyundai Excel	209
Mazda Protege	140
Nissan Sentra	158
Plymouth Sundance	141
Subaru Impreza	136
Toyota Corolla	143
Toyota Tercel	157
Volkswagen Jetta	132
Average	144
2–DOOR CARS	
Large	
Ford Thunderbird	96
Mercury Cougar	96
Average	90
Midsize	
Acura Integra	98
Chevrolet Beretta	116

Model	Injury
2-DOOR CARS	
Midsize	
Chevrolet Cavalier	124
Chevrolet Cavalier Convertible	100
Chevrolet Lumina	91
Chrysler LeBaron Convertible	103
Ford Probe	117
Ford Tempo	129
Honda Accord	103
Honda Civic	106
Honda Civic Coupe	143
Honda Prelude	118
Mazda MX-5	100
Mercury Topaz	131
Pontiac Grand Am	106
Pontiac Grand Prix	72
Pontiac Sunbird	131
Pontiac Sunbird Convertible	98
Toyota Celica	105
Average	110
Small	
Dodge Shadow	141
Eagle Talon	122
Eagle Talon 4WD	76
Ford Escort	133
Geo Metro	160
Hyundai Excel	172
Hyundai Scoupe	233
Mazda 323	126
Mitsubishi Eclipse	139
Nissan Sentra	137
Plymouth Laser	124
Plymouth Sundance	130
Saturn SC	98

Model	Injury
2-DOOR CARS	
Small	
Toyota Paseo	163
Toyota Tercel	156
Average	141
SPORTS CARS	
Midsize	
Chevrolet Camaro	113
Ford Mustang	128
Pontiac Firebird	103
Subaru SVX 4WD	80
Average	112
Small	
Chevrolet Corvette	71
Chevrolet Corvette Convertible	61
Dodge Stealth	104
Honda Civic Del Sol Convertible	109
Mazda MX-5 Miata Convertible	93
Mazda RX-7	79
Mercedes S Class Convertible	43
Mercury Capri Convertible	116
Mitsubishi 3000GT	90
Nissan 300ZX	82
Saab 900 Convertible	74
Toyota MR2	106
Average	88
PICKUP TRUCKS	
Standard	
Chevrolet 1500	71
Chevrolet 1500 4x4	51
Chevrolet 2500	56
Chevrolet 2500 4x4	44

Model	Injury
PICKUP TRUCKS	
Standard	
Chevrolet 3500	62
Chevrolet 3500 4x4	61
Dodge Ram 1500	79
Dodge Ram 1500 4x4	50
Ford F-150	73
Ford F-150 4x4	53
Ford F-250	48
Ford F-250 4x4	50
Ford F-350	52
Ford F-350 4x4	43
GMC 1500	64
GMC 1500 4x4	52
GMC 2500 4x4	40
Average	59
Small	
Chevrolet S-10	96
Chevrolet S-10 4x4	70
Dodge Dakota	80
Ford Ranger	90
Ford Ranger 4x4	75
GMC	87
GMC 4x4	77
Isuzu	115
Mazda	97
Mazda 4x4	80
Mitsubishi	112
Nissan	106
Nissan 4x4	83
Toyota	111
Toyota 4x4	90
Average	91

Model	Injury
UTILITY VEHICLES	
Large	
Chevrolet Suburban 1500	42
Chevrolet Suburban 1500 4x4	43
GMC Suburban 1500	45
GMC Suburban 1500 4x4	52
Average	44
Intermediate	
GMC Yukon 4x4	45
Toyota Land Cruiser	52
Chevrolet K1500 Blazer	54
Ford Explorer 2-door 4x4	60
Ford Explorer 4-door 4x4	62
Jeep Grand Cherokee 4-door 4x4	62
Ford Explorer 4x4	63
Jeep Cherokee 4-door 4x4	72
Isuzu Trooper 4-door 4x4	74
GMC Jimmy 2-door 4x4	75
Jeep Cherokee 2-door 4x4	77
Mazda Navajo 2-door 4x4	78
Jeep Grand Cherokee 4-door	79
Ford Explorer 2-door	81
GMC Jimmy 4-door 4x4	83
Oldsmobile Bravada 4-door 4x4	83
Nissan Pathfinder 4-door 4x4	89
Chevrolet Blazer 4-door 4x4	92
Jeep Cherokee 4-door	94
Chevrolet Blazer 2-door 4x4	96
Chevrolet S-10 Blazer 4-door	96
Toyota 4-Runner 4-door 4x4	97
Jeep Cherokee 2-door	101
Chevrolet S-10 Blazer 2-door	103
GMC 515 Jimmy 4-door	103
Toyota 4-Runner 4-door	105

Model	Injury
UTILITY VEHICLES	
Intermediate	
Isuzu Rodeo 4-door 4x4	106
Isuzu Rodeo 4x4	110
Nissan Pathfinder 4-door	113
Average	76
Small	
Geo Tracker	162
Geo Tracker 4x4	143
Isuzu Amigo	151
Jeep Wrangler	89
Suzuki Sidekick 4-door 4x4	121
Average	113
WAGONS AND VANS	
Large	
Buick Estate Wagon	41
Chevrolet Astro	84
Chevrolet Caprice	56
Chevrolet Lumina APV	80
Chrysler Town & Country	51
Dodge Caravan	74
Dodge Caravan 4WD	52
Ford Aerostar	90
Ford Aerostar 4WD	72
Mazda MPV	128
Mercury Villager	57
Nissan Quest	76
Plymouth Voyager	71
Pontiac Trans Sport	58
Toyota Previa	86
Toyota Previa 4WD	58
Average	75

Model	Injury
WAGONS AND VANS	
Midsize	
Chevrolet Cavalier	93
Ford Taurus	72
Mercury Sable	58
Saturn SW	78
Subaru Legacy 4WD	74
Toyota Camry	69
Average	78
Small	
Ford Escort	115
Subaru Loyale 4WD	81
Toyota Corolla •	104
Average	100
LUXURY CARS	
Large	
Acura Legend 4-door	69
Acura Legend 2-door	88
Cadillac Brougham	60
Cadillac DeVille	47
Cadillac Seville	55
Chrysler LHS	52
Infiniti Q45	61
Jaguar XJ	53
Lexus LS 400	53
Lincoln Mark VIII	67
Lincoln Town Car	63
Mazda 929	83
Mercedes E Class 4-door	79
Mercedes S Class long wheelbase	42
Mercedes S Class short wheelbase	60
Average	64

Model	Injury
LUXURY CARS	
Midsize	
Audi 100 4-door	67
BMW 3 series 2-door	99
BMW 3 series 4-door	98
BMW 5 series 4-door	70
Cadillac Eldorado	62
Infiniti J30	86
Lexus GS 300	88
Lexus SC 300/400	61
Lincoln Continental	73
Saab 9000	58
Volvo 940/960 Station Wagon	56
Volvo 960/940 4-door	77
Average	76

APPENDIX C

Rating the Crash Tests

Each year the National Highway Traffic Safety Administration conducts crash tests by ramming cars into a barrier at 35 MPH. From the damage to the crash test dummies, they deduce what injuries would have resulted to the driver and passenger. Each vehicle gets a rating for driver and passenger from one star (more than a 45% chance of a life-threatening injury) to five stars (less than a 10% chance of such an injury). The vehicles for which results were available are listed below with their star ratings.

Name	Driver	Passenger
SMALL CARS		
Geo Metro	4	4
Ford Aspire	4	4
Honda Civic	4	5
Hyundai Accent	5	4
Mazda MX-5 Miata	4	3
Mitsubishi Mirage	3	3

Name	Driver	Passenger
SMALL CARS		
Nissan Sentra	4	4
Saturn Sl	4	4
Toyota Tercel	3	4
Acura Integra	4	3
Chevrolet Cavalier	3	3
Chevrolet Corsica	3	2
Dodge Avenger	5	5
Dodge Neon	4	4
Ford Escort	4	4
Ford Probe	5	4
Honda Accord	4	3
Hyundai Sonata	3	4
Mazda 626	4	5
Mitsubishi Eclipse	4	4
Mitsubishi Galant	N.A.	4
Nissan 240SX	3	4
Nissan Altima	4	4
Nissan Maxima	4	3
Pontiac Grand Am	4	4
Subaru Impreza	4	4
Subaru Legacy	4	4
Toyota Camry	4	5
Toyota Corolla	4	4
Volkswagen Jetta	3	3
MIDSIZE CARS		
Acura TL	4	4
Audi A4	4	5
Audi A6	5	5
BMW 328	4	4
Buick Century	4	4
Chevrolet Camaro	5	5
Chevrolet Lumina	5	4
Chevrolet Monte Carlo	4	4

Name	Driver	Passenger
MIDSIZE CARS		
Dodge Intrepid	4	4
Dodge Stratus	3	N.A.
Ford Contour	5	4
Ford Mustang	4	4
Ford Mustang Convertible	5	5
Ford Taurus	4	4
Ford Thunderbird	5	5
Honda Odyssey	4	4
Lexus ES 300	5	3
Mazda Millenia	4	5
Mercedes-Benz C220	4	4
Pontiac Grand Prix	4	3
Saab 900	4	4
Toyota Avalon	4	5
Toyota Camry	4	3
Volkswagen Passat	4	4
Volvo 850	5	4
LARGE CARS		
Chevrolet Caprice	4	2
Chrysler New Yorker	4	4
Ford Crown Victoria	5	5
Infiniti J30	4	4
Lexus GS 300	3	3
Oldsmobile Aurora	3	3
Pontiac Bonneville	5	3
SPORT UTILITIES		
Chevrolet S-10 Blazer	3	1
Chevrolet Tahoe	4	3
Ford Bronco	5	5
Ford Explorer	4	4
Geo Tracker	2	3
Isuzu Rodeo	4	3

Name	Driver	Passenger
SPORT UTILITIES		
Jeep Cherokee	4	4
Jeep Wrangler	2	4
Land Rover Discovery	3	3
Toyota 4-Runner	3	3
PICKUPS		
Chevrolet S-10	3	1
Dodge Dakota	5	4
Dodge Ram	5	N.A.
Ford F-150	5	5
Ford Ranger	4	4
Mitsubishi	3	3
Toyota T-100	4	5
Toyota Tacoma	2	3
MINIVANS		
Chevrolet Astro	3	3
Dodge Grand Caravan	3	4
Dodge Ram Van	3	4
Ford Aerostar	4	3
Ford Econoline	4	3
Ford WindStar	5	5
Mercury Villager	4	3
Pontiac Trans Sport	5	3
Toyota Previa	4	3

APPENDIX D

How Much Loan for the Payments

This table will help you determine how much car you can afford within your budget in connection with the worksheet in Chapter 5. Find the appropriate table for the likely length of your loan (three, four, or five years). Check the top row until you find the monthly payment you can afford. Then look in the left-hand column to find the closest figure to recent car loan interest rate in your area. Where your payments match the interest rate, that figure will tell you how much you will be able to borrow.

AUTO LOAN QUALIFICATION TABLE:
HOW MUCH AUTO LOAN CAN I BORROW? (36 MONTHS)

Rate %	36 Months	36 Months	36 Months	36 Months	36 Months	36 Months	36 Months	36 Months	36 Months
$ payment	$100	$150	$200	$250	$300	$350	$400	$450	$500
11.00	$3,054	$4,582	$6,109	$7,636	$9,163	$10,691	$12,218	$13,745	$15,272
10.75	$3,066	$4,598	$6,131	$7,664	$9,197	$10,729	$12,262	$13,795	$15,328
10.50	$3,077	$4,615	$6,153	$7,692	$9,230	$10,768	$12,307	$13,845	$15,383
10.25	$3,088	$4,632	$6,176	$7,720	$9,264	$10,808	$12,351	$13,895	$15,439
10.00	$3,099	$4,649	$6,198	$7,748	$9,297	$10,847	$12,397	$13,946	$15,496
9.75	$3,110	$4,666	$6,221	$7,776	$9,331	$10,886	$12,442	$13,997	$15,552
9.50	$3,122	$4,683	$6,244	$7,804	$9,365	$10,926	$12,487	$14,048	$15,609
9.25	$3,133	$4,700	$6,266	$7,833	$9,400	$10,966	$12,533	$14,099	$15,666
9.00	$3,145	$4,717	$6,289	$7,862	$9,434	$11,006	$12,579	$14,151	$15,723
8.75	$3,156	$4,734	$6,312	$7,891	$9,469	$11,047	$12,625	$14,203	$15,781
8.50	$3,168	$4,752	$6,336	$7,920	$9,503	$11,087	$12,671	$14,255	$15,839
8.25	$3,179	$4,769	$6,359	$7,949	$9,538	$11,128	$12,718	$14,308	$15,897
8.00	$3,191	$4,787	$6,382	$7,978	$9,574	$11,169	$12,765	$14,360	$15,956
7.75	$3,203	$4,804	$6,406	$8,007	$9,609	$11,210	$12,812	$14,413	$16,015
7.50	$3,215	$4,822	$6,430	$8,037	$9,644	$11,252	$12,859	$14,467	$16,074
7.25	$3,227	$4,840	$6,453	$8,067	$9,680	$11,293	$12,907	$14,520	$16,133
7.00	$3,239	$4,858	$6,477	$8,097	$9,716	$11,335	$12,955	$14,574	$16,193
6.75	$3,251	$4,876	$6,501	$8,127	$9,752	$11,377	$13,003	$14,628	$16,253
6.50	$3,263	$4,894	$6,525	$8,157	$9,788	$11,420	$13,051	$14,682	$16,314
6.25	$3,275	$4,912	$6,550	$8,187	$9,825	$11,462	$13,100	$14,737	$16,374
6.00	$3,287	$4,931	$6,574	$8,218	$9,861	$11,505	$13,148	$14,792	$16,436

AUTO LOAN QUALIFICATION TABLE:
HOW MUCH AUTO LOAN CAN I BORROW? (48 MONTHS)

Rate %	48 Months	48 Months	48 Months	48 Months	48 Months	48 Months	48 Months	48 Months	48 Months
$ payment	$100	$150	$200	$250	$300	$350	$400	$450	$500
11.00	$3,869	$5,804	$7,738	$9,673	$11,607	$13,542	$15,477	$17,411	$19,346
10.75	$3,887	$5,831	$7,775	$9,718	$11,662	$13,606	$15,549	$17,493	$19,437
10.50	$3,906	$5,859	$7,811	$9,764	$11,717	$13,670	$15,623	$17,576	$19,529
10.25	$3,924	$5,886	$7,848	$9,811	$11,773	$13,735	$15,697	$17,659	$19,621
10.00	$3,943	$5,914	$7,886	$9,857	$11,828	$13,800	$15,771	$17,743	$19,714
9.75	$3,962	$5,942	$7,923	$9,904	$11,885	$13,865	$15,846	$17,827	$19,808
9.50	$3,980	$5,971	$7,961	$9,951	$11,941	$13,931	$15,922	$17,912	$19,902
9.25	$3,999	$5,999	$7,999	$9,998	$11,998	$13,998	$15,997	$17,997	$19,997
9.00	$4,018	$6,028	$8,037	$10,046	$12,055	$14,065	$16,074	$18,083	$20,092
8.75	$4,038	$6,057	$8,075	$10,094	$12,113	$14,132	$16,151	$18,170	$20,189
8.50	$4,057	$6,086	$8,114	$10,143	$12,171	$14,200	$16,228	$18,257	$20,285
8.25	$4,077	$6,115	$8,153	$10,191	$12,230	$14,268	$16,306	$18,345	$20,383
8.00	$4,096	$6,144	$8,192	$10,240	$12,289	$14,337	$16,385	$18,433	$20,481
7.75	$4,116	$6,174	$8,232	$10,290	$12,348	$14,406	$16,464	$18,522	$20,580
7.50	$4,136	$6,204	$8,272	$10,340	$12,407	$14,475	$16,543	$18,611	$20,679
7.25	$4,156	$6,234	$8,312	$10,390	$12,468	$14,546	$16,623	$18,701	$20,779
7.00	$4,176	$6,264	$8,352	$10,440	$12,528	$14,616	$16,704	$18,792	$20,880
6.75	$4,196	$6,294	$8,393	$10,491	$12,589	$14,687	$16,785	$18,883	$20,982
6.50	$4,217	$6,325	$8,433	$10,542	$12,650	$14,759	$16,867	$18,975	$21,084
6.25	$4,237	$6,356	$8,475	$10,593	$12,712	$14,831	$16,949	$19,068	$21,187
6.00	$4,258	$6,387	$8,516	$10,645	$12,774	$14,903	$17,032	$19,161	$21,290

AUTO LOAN QUALIFICATION TABLE:
HOW MUCH AUTO LOAN CAN I BORROW? (60 MONTHS)

Rate %	60 Months	60 Months	60 Months	60 Months	60 Months	60 Months	60 Months	60 Months	60 Months
$ payment	$100	$150	$200	$250	$300	$350	$400	$450	$500
11.00	$4,599	$6,899	$9,199	$11,498	$13,798	$16,098	$18,397	$20,697	$22,997
10.75	$4,626	$6,939	$9,252	$11,564	$13,877	$16,190	$18,503	$20,816	$23,129
10.50	$4,652	$6,979	$9,305	$11,631	$13,957	$16,284	$18,610	$20,936	$23,262
10.25	$4,679	$7,019	$9,359	$11,698	$14,038	$16,378	$18,718	$21,057	$23,397
10.00	$4,707	$7,060	$9,413	$11,766	$14,120	$16,473	$18,826	$21,179	$23,533
9.75	$4,734	$7,101	$9,468	$11,835	$14,202	$16,569	$18,936	$21,303	$23,669
9.50	$4,761	$7,142	$9,523	$11,904	$14,284	$16,665	$19,046	$21,427	$23,807
9.25	$4,789	$7,184	$9,579	$11,973	$14,368	$16,763	$19,157	$21,552	$23,946
9.00	$4,817	$7,226	$9,635	$12,043	$14,452	$16,861	$19,269	$21,678	$24,087
8.75	$4,846	$7,268	$9,691	$12,114	$14,537	$16,960	$19,382	$21,805	$24,228
8.50	$4,874	$7,311	$9,748	$12,185	$14,622	$17,059	$19,496	$21,933	$24,371
8.25	$4,903	$7,354	$9,806	$12,257	$14,709	$17,160	$19,611	$22,063	$24,514
8.00	$4,932	$7,398	$9,864	$12,330	$14,796	$17,261	$19,727	$22,193	$24,659
7.75	$4,961	$7,442	$9,922	$12,403	$14,883	$17,364	$19,844	$22,325	$24,805
7.50	$4,991	$7,486	$9,981	$12,476	$14,972	$17,467	$19,962	$22,457	$24,953
7.25	$5,020	$7,530	$10,040	$12,551	$15,061	$17,571	$20,081	$22,591	$25,101
7.00	$5,050	$7,575	$10,100	$12,625	$15,151	$17,676	$20,201	$22,726	$25,251
6.75	$5,080	$7,621	$10,161	$12,701	$15,241	$17,781	$20,322	$22,862	$25,402
6.50	$5,111	$7,666	$10,222	$12,777	$15,333	$17,888	$20,443	$22,999	$25,554
6.25	$5,142	$7,712	$10,283	$12,854	$15,425	$17,996	$20,566	$23,137	$25,708
6.00	$5,173	$7,759	$10,345	$12,931	$15,518	$18,104	$20,690	$23,276	$25,863

Source: HSH Associates

INDEX

AAA. *See* American Automobile Association

ABS. *See* Automatic braking system

Accidents. *See* Car crashes; Safety issues

Acquisition fees, 112

Acura
consumer satisfaction, 122
crash test results, by model, 190
injury claims, by model, 179, 181, 187
insurance costs, by model, 171, 172, 174,
175
warranties, 160

Acura Legend, 40, 41, 179, 187

Advertising, 7–8

Advertising fee, dealer, 72, 126, 165

Air bags, 31–32, 38

American Automobile Association (AAA),
93, 94, 119–20, 158

America Online, 68

Annual percentage rate (APR), 78, 165

Anticorrosion warranties, 136

Antitheft devices, 31, 41–42

APR. *See* Annual percentage rate

Arbitration programs, 156, 158

ArmChair Compare (research service), 67

Audi
consumer satisfaction, 122
crash test results, by model, 190

injury claims, by model, 188
insurance costs, by model, 174

Audi A6, 34, 174, 190

AutoAdvisor (buying service), 9, 90, 91

Auto brokers, 95–96, 157

Auto-by-Tel (dealer referral service), 94–95

Auto malls, 100, 146–47

Automatic braking system (ABS), 38

Automatic electronic cutoff switches, 31,
41–42

Automobile (magazine), 68

Automobile clubs
arbitration programs, 158
dealer referral services, 93–94
service department ratings, 119–20

Automobile Consumer Services, 91

Automobile insurance. *See* Insurance

Automobile loans, 76–83
borrowing capacity determination, 61–63
monthly payment calculation, 79–81
qualification calculation, 193–96
sources for, 76–79, 101
used car financing, 82–83, 139

Automobile selection. *See* Vehicle selection

Automobile shows, 73–74

Automobile theft. *See* Car theft

Automotive Lease Guide, 106, 107, 108

197

Automotive News (newspaper), 66
Automotive Service Excellence (ASE)
　certification, 119, 120
AutoNation (superstore), 146
Autonet (on-line service), 68
Auto rentals. *See* Rental companies
Autos, used. *See* Used cars
Avis Corporation, 75

Baby car seats, 32
Back-end options, 133–37, 165
Banks, car financing, 76, 77–78, 82
Better Business Bureau, 95, 119, 158
BMW
　consumer satisfaction, 122
　crash test results, by model, 190
　injury claims, by model, 188
　insurance costs, by model, 174
　warranties, 160
BMW 3 series, 37, 188
BMW 300i series, 40, 41
BMW Z3, 69
Borrowing capacity, 61–63
Brokers, 95–96, 157
Budget Rent-a-Car, 75
Buick
　consumer satisfaction, 122
　crash test results, by model, 190
　injury claims, by model, 179, 180, 186
　insurance costs, by model, 171, 172, 174
Buick Century Special, 18, 171, 180, 190
Buick LeSabre, 36, 41, 172, 174, 179
Buick Park Avenue, 29, 36, 41, 55, 174, 179
Buick Regal, 36, 41, 171, 172, 180
Buick Skylark, 41, 171
Business uses, 25–26, 51–52

Cadillac, 18, 28–29
　consumer satisfaction, 122
　injury claims, by model, 187, 188
　insurance costs, by model, 175
　warranties, 160
Cadillac DeVille, 37, 55, 175, 187
Cadillac Seville, 55, 175, 187
Capital cost reduction, 47, 61, 167
Capitalized cost, 104, 105, 109, 110, 164,
　166–67
Car and Driver (magazine), 22, 68
Car Bargains (buying service), 92, 93, 94, 130

Car-buying services, 87–96; *See also specific*
　buying services
Car Choice (superstore), 146
Car crashes
　air bags and, 31–32, 38
　collision claims, 36
　injury claims, 35–38, 179–88
　safety test results, 33–35, 189–92
　size as safety factor, 33
Car crash testing. *See* Crash test results
Car Deals (newsletter), 66, 67
Cargo space
　by model categories, 10–17
　vehicle selection and, 21–23
Car loans. *See* Automobile loans
CarMax (superstore), 50, 99, 141, 145–46
Car rentals. *See* Rental companies
Cars, used. *See* Used cars
Car selection. *See* Vehicle selection
Car shows, 73–74
CarSource (buying service), 90
Car theft, 39–42
　antitheft devices, 31, 41–42
　commuter cars and, 24
　insurance costs and, 40
　most stolen models, 31, 40–41
Certification programs (used car), 49, 115,
　141, 148
Chart Software, 107
Chevrolet
　crash test results, by model, 190, 191, 192
　injury claims, by model, 179, 180, 181–82,
　　183, 183–84, 185, 186, 187
　insurance costs, by model, 169, 171, 172,
　　175–76, 177
　value-pricing plans, 102
Chevrolet Astro, 37, 177, 186, 192
Chevrolet Camaro, 34, 42, 169, 171, 183, 190
Chevrolet Corvette, 42, 175, 183
Chevrolet Lumina, 25, 41, 171, 176, 180, 182,
　186, 190
Chevrolet Suburban, 65, 69, 175, 185
Chevrolet T-100 series 4WD, 38
Children, air bag fatalities, 32
Child safety seats, 32
Chop shops, 39
Chrysler Concorde, 36, 69, 171, 179
Chrysler Corporation, 10, 99
　antitheft devices, 42
　crash test results, by model, 191
　injury claims, by model, 179, 182, 186, 187

insurance costs, by model, 171, 172, 174
minivan models, 15, 26
used car fraud, 142
Chrysler LHS, 37, 187
Chrysler New Yorker, 34, 174, 179, 191
Chrysler Sebring, 34, 171, 172
Chrysler Town and Country, 26, 37, 55, 176, 186
Circuit City, 99, 141, 145
Closed-end leases, 45, 167
Club, The (antitheft device), 41
CNW Marketing/Research, 139
Collision insurance
claim incidence, 36
cost of, 54–55
Commuting considerations, 24–25
Compact cars
crash test results, by model, 34
See also Small cars
Comprehensive insurance coverage, 40, 54–55
CompuServe, 68
Consumer Reports (magazine), 143, 145
Consumer Reports Annual Auto Issue, 143
Consumer satisfaction, 98, 118, 122
Consumer satisfaction index (CSI), 117–18
Costs. See Dealer's cost; Prices
Crashes. See Car crashes
Crash test results, 33–35, 189–92
Credit. See Automobile loans; Financing
Credit life insurance, 135–36
Credit Union National Association, 79
Credit unions, 67, 76–77, 79, 82, 104
CSI. See Consumer satisfaction index
Cutoff switches, 31, 41–42

Dealer financing, 81–82, 132, 133–34
Dealer incentives, 65–66, 71–72, 91
Dealer referral, 93–95
Dealers
"lemon" cars and, 155–56
new car, 147–48
service departments, 116–22, 148, 155
used car, 148
See also Auto malls; One-price dealers; Superstores
Dealer's cost, 64–66, 69–70, 72–73
Dealer swaps, 129–30, 165
Deal negotiation
car-buying services, 88, 90–96
on leased cars, 109–12

negotiating tips, 123–33, 163–64
one-price dealers, 72–73, 88, 89–90, 97–102
preparation for, 69–75, 162–63
purchase add-ons, 133–37, 165
on used cars, 150–51, 153
Deposits, 132
Depreciation, 57, 104, 152, 167
Destination charges, 166
Detailing, 59
Disposition fees, 112
Dodge
crash test results, by model, 190, 191, 192
injury claims, by model, 179, 180, 181, 182, 183, 184, 186
insurance costs, by model, 169, 171, 172, 176, 177
Dodge Avenger, 34, 169, 171, 190
Dodge Caravan, 26, 37, 56, 176, 186, 192
Dodge Dakota, 35, 177, 184, 192
Dodge Intrepid, 36, 171, 172, 179, 191
Dohring Company, 27, 87, 89
Downey, Peg, 63
Down payments, 47, 61, 161

Eagle
injury claims, by model, 179, 182
insurance costs, by model, 169, 171, 173
Eagle Talon, 36, 169, 171, 173, 182
Eagle Vision, 36, 171, 173, 179
Early termination (leasing), 167
Eaton, Robert, 8
Edmund's (guide publisher), Internet site, 68, 94
Edmund's New Car Prices (book), 23, 66
Edmund's New Pickup, Van and Sport Utility Prices (book), 66
Edmund's Used Cars Price and Ratings (book), 58, 114, 143, 144
Excess wear and tear fees, 112–13
Expert Lease (software), 107
Extended warranties, 135, 161, 164

Fabric protection, 136
Factory orders, 91, 93
Family transportation, 26
Federal Reserve Board, 105
Fees
acquisition, 112
dealer advertising, 72, 126, 165

(Fees, continued)
disposition, 112
excess mileage charges, 108–9, 167
excess wear and tear, 112–13
freight/destination charges, 53, 72, 126, 166
Fighting Chance (research service), 67
Financing, 60–63, 76–83
borrowing capacity determination, 61–63
dealer, 81–82, 132, 133–34
down payments, 47, 61, 161
loan qualification calculation, 193–96
monthly payment calculation, 79–81
planning strategy, 160–61
sources for, 76–79, 101
of used cars, 82–83, 139
See also Leasing
Fitzharris, Bob, 99, 100
Ford Aerostar, 37, 41, 176, 186, 192
Ford Aspire, 34, 169, 189
Ford Crown Victoria, 34, 173, 179, 191
Ford E-150 Club Wagon, 41
Ford Escort, 36, 170, 181, 182, 187, 190
Ford Explorer, 18, 22, 27, 35, 37, 40, 56, 176, 185, 191
Ford F-150, 28, 177, 184, 192
Ford Motor Company
antitheft devices, 42
consumer satisfaction, 118–19, 122
crash test results, by model, 189, 190, 191, 192
injury claims, by model, 179, 180, 181, 182, 183, 184, 185, 186, 187
insurance costs, by model, 169–70, 171, 173, 176, 177
Ford Motor Credit, 76, 104
Ford Mustang, 34, 40, 42, 55, 171, 173, 183, 191
Ford Probe, 34, 170, 171, 182, 190
Ford Ranger, 35, 38, 177, 184, 192
Ford Taurus, 56, 171, 173, 180, 187, 191
Ford Thunderbird, 34, 36, 171, 181, 191
Ford Windstar, 26, 35, 176, 192
Four-wheel drive, 18; *See also* Sport utility vehicles
Freight charges, 53, 72, 126, 166
Fricke, Philip, 31

Gap insurance, 109
Gas mileage
commuting considerations, 24, 25
by model categories, 10–17

General Electric Capital, 104
General Motors Acceptance Corporation, 76, 104
General Motors Corporation, 13
anticorrosion warranties, 136
antitheft devices, 42
Saturn division, 99
value-pricing plans, 73, 101–2
See also specific car divisions
Geo Metro, 24, 34, 55, 170, 181, 182, 189
Geo Prizm, 170, 181
Geo Tracker, 176, 186, 191
GMC
injury claims, by model, 184, 185
insurance costs, by model, 176, 177
GMC T-15 series, 38
GMC Yukon, 28, 37, 176, 185
Goldberg, Linda Lee, 90
Gumbinger, Keith, 83

Haggling. *See* Deal negotiation
Hart, Charles, 113, 114
Hazelbaker, Kim, 42
Hertz Corporation, 75
Highway Loss Data Institute, 33, 35, 40, 179
Holdback, 65, 127, 166
Home-equity loans, 77
Honda
consumer satisfaction, 122
crash test results, by model, 189, 190, 191
injury claims, by model, 180, 182, 183
insurance costs, by model, 170, 171, 173, 176
residual value and, 104
Honda Accord, 18, 40, 171, 173, 180, 182, 190
Honda Civic, 24, 34, 36, 170, 171, 180, 182, 183, 189
Honda Odyssey, 35, 176, 191
Hyundai
crash test results, by model, 189, 190
injury claims, by model, 180, 181, 182
insurance costs, by model, 170, 171
Hyundai Excel, 36, 181, 182
Hyundai Scoupe, 36, 182
Hyundai Sonata, 36, 170, 171, 180, 190

Idema, Matt, 27
Infant car seats, 32

Infiniti
consumer satisfaction, 122
crash test results, by model, 191
injury claims, by model, 180, 187, 188
insurance costs, by model, 173, 174, 175
invoice price reductions, 102
used-car warranties, 49, 115, 148
Infiniti J30, 29, 34, 37, 188, 191
Injury claims, by car model, 36–38, 179–88
Insurance
antitheft device discounts, 31, 41–42
car safety as factor, 30–31
collision claims, 36
comprehensive coverage, 40
costs, by car model, 55–56, 169–77
injury claims, 35–38, 179–88
leased cars and, 109
on used cars, 49
vehicle selection and, 10, 54–56
See also Credit life insurance
Insurance Institute for Highway Safety, 31
Insurance Services Office, 55
Intellichoice (research firm), 56, 57, 67
Interest rates. See Automobile loans
Internet
antitheft device information, 42
car specifications information, 23
dealer referral services, 94–95
price research, 68, 144
used-car value information, 58
Invoice cost, 166
Invoice price, 65–66, 69–70, 72–73, 92–93,
100, 126, 164
Isuzu
crash test results, by model, 191
injury claims, by model, 184, 185, 186
insurance costs, by model, 176
Isuzu Amigo, 186
Isuzu Pickup, 38, 184
Isuzu Rodeo, 37, 186, 191
Isuzu Trooper, 176, 185

Jaguar
injury claims, by model, 187
insurance costs, by model, 175
new-car warranties, 160
used-car warranties, 49, 115, 148
J. D. Power and Company, 44, 73, 98, 122,
139, 143
Jeep Cherokee, 35, 176, 185, 192

Jeep Grand Cherokee, 22, 27, 37, 176, 185
Jeep Wrangler, 186, 192

Kalmus, Dave, 27, 50
Karbon, Jerry, 64
Knapp, Ashly, 9, 29

Land Rover, 176, 192
Large cars
category overview, 12–13
crash test results, by model, 34, 191
injury claims, by model, 36, 179–80, 181,
186, 187
insurance costs, by model, 174–75
Lassus, Diahann, 54, 161
Leasing, 103–15
analysis software, 107–8
business uses and, 25–26, 51–52
buying vs., 43–52
capital cost reduction, 47, 61, 167
capitalized cost, 104, 105, 109, 110, 164,
166–67
closed-end, 45, 167
deal negotiation, 109–12
depreciation considerations, 57, 167
early termination, 167
excess mileage charges, 108–9, 167
fees incurred, 112–13
gap insurance, 109
"lemon laws" and, 157
lessee/lessor, 167
money factor, 104, 109, 110
needs assessment, 44–45
payment calculation, 61–63
purchase options, 113–14, 168
residual value, 46, 104, 106, 109, 110, 168
subsidized, 12, 44, 67, 103, 104, 106
of used cars, 49–50, 114–15
warranties and, 108
"Lemon laws," 154, 156, 157–58, 164
Levy, Peter, 57
Lexus
consumer satisfaction, 122
crash test results, by model, 191
injury claims, by model, 180, 187, 188
insurance costs, by model, 174, 175
new-car warranties, 160
used-car warranties, 49, 115, 141, 148
Lexus GS 300, 37, 41, 188, 191

Lexus LS 400, 37, 187
Liability insurance, 54
Lincoln
 consumer satisfaction, 122
 injury claims, by model, 187, 188
 insurance costs, by model, 175
Lincoln Town Car, 18, 28, 175, 187
List price. *See* Manufacturer's suggested retail
 price
Litvak, Ronald, 69
Loaner cars, 121
Loans. *See* Automobile loans; Financing
Lujack's Northpark Auto Plaza, 100
Luxury cars
 antitheft devices, 42
 best buys, 29
 category overview, 13–14
 deal negotiation, 70
 import image vs. domestic, 28–29
 injury claims, by model, 37, 187–88
 maintenance costs, 56
 as used cars, 49–50, 140
Luxury tax, 140

Maintenance
 dealer service, 116–22
 long-term car care, 159–60
 of used cars, 50
 vehicle selection and, 10, 56
 See also Warranties
Manufacturers
 car financing, 76
 car leasing, 105
 car specifications information, 23
 consumer satisfaction index, 117–18
 dealer incentives, 65–66
 Internet sites, 23, 68
 new-car warranties, 56–57, 108, 116, 134
 used-car certification, 49, 115, 141, 148
 See also specific manufacturers
Manufacturer's suggested retail price
 (MSRP), 65, 166
Mauro Auto Mall, 100, 147
Mazda
 consumer satisfaction, 122
 crash test results, by model, 189, 190, 191
 injury claims, by model, 180, 181, 182, 183,
  184, 185, 186, 187
 insurance costs, by model, 170, 171, 173,
  174, 175, 177

Mazda 626, 34, 171, 173, 180, 190
Mazda Millenia, 25, 174, 175, 191
Mazda MPV, 18, 37, 177, 186
Mazda Pickup, 38, 184
Mercedes-Benz
 consumer satisfaction, 122
 crash test results, by model, 191
 injury claims, by model, 183, 187
 insurance costs, by model, 174, 175
 new-car warranties, 160
 residual value and, 104
 used-car warranties, 49, 115, 141, 148
Mercedes E-320, 29, 175
Mercedes S Class, 37, 40, 183, 187
Mercedes SL Class, 40, 175
Mercury
 consumer satisfaction, 122
 crash test results, by model, 192
 injury claims, by model, 180, 181, 182,
  183, 186, 187
 insurance costs, by model, 170, 171, 173,
  177
Mercury Cougar, 36, 171, 181
Mercury Sable, 56, 171, 173, 180, 187
Mercury Villager, 37, 177, 186, 192
Midsize cars
 category overview, 11–12
 crash test results, by model, 34, 190–91
 injury claims, by model, 36, 180–82, 183,
  187, 188
 insurance costs, by model, 171–73
Mileage
 as leasing factor, 108–9, 167
 as value factor, 58
 See also Gas mileage
Minivans
 cargo space, 22
 category overview, 15
 crash test results, by model, 35, 192
 family transportation and, 26
 gas mileage, 26
 injury claims, by model, 37, 186–87
 insurance costs, by model, 176–77
 residual value and, 104
Mitsubishi, 10
 consumer satisfaction, 122
 crash test results, by model, 189, 190, 192
 injury claims, by model, 180, 182, 183, 184
 insurance costs, by model, 170, 172, 173,
  174, 176, 177
Mitsubishi B2300, 28

Mitsubishi Montero, 31, 35, 40, 176
Mitsubishi Pickup, 38, 177, 184, 192
Model selection. *See* Vehicle selection
Money (magazine), 66
Money factor, 104, 109, 110
Monthly payment calculation, 79–81
MSRP. *See* Manufacturer's suggested retail
    price

NADA. *See* National Auto Dealers Association
NADA Official Used Car Guide, 58, 101, 114,
    144, 166
National Association of Buyers' Agents, 90
National Auto Dealers Association (NADA),
    144
National Highway Traffic Safety
    Administration (NHTSA), 32, 33, 34,
    189
National Institute for Automotive Service
    Excellence, 119
National Insurance Crime Bureau, 39, 40, 42
Negotiation. *See* Deal negotiation
NHTSA. *See* National Highway Traffic Safety
    Administration
Nissan
    consumer satisfaction, 122
    crash test results, by model, 190
    injury claims, by model, 180, 181, 182, 183,
        184, 185, 186
    insurance costs, by model, 170, 172, 173,
        174, 177
    used-car warranties, 49, 141, 148
    See also Infiniti
Nissan Altima, 25, 36, 172, 173, 180, 190
Nissan Maxima, 25, 173, 174, 180, 190
Nissan Pathfinder, 27–28, 37, 185, 186
Nissan Pickup, 38, 184
Nissan Sentra, 34, 170, 172, 181, 182, 190
Nissan 300ZX, 41, 183
Nolan, Kathy, 98–99
Northstar engine, 29

Oldsmobile
    consumer satisfaction, 122
    crash test results, by model, 191
    injury claims, by model, 180, 185
    insurance costs, by model, 170, 172, 173,
        174, 177
    value-pricing plans, 73, 101–2

Oldsmobile Cutlass Supreme, 36, 40, 172,
    173, 180
Oldsmobile 98, 36, 174, 180
One-price dealers, 88, 89–90, 97–102
    dealer markup, 72–73
    maintenance considerations, 117
    used car, 99–100, 145, 147
On-line services, 68

Passenger seating
    by model category, 10–17
    vehicle selection and, 21
Passive antitheft systems, 41–42
Pass-key systems, 42
Pickup trucks
    best buys, 28
    category overview, 17
    crash test results, by model, 35, 192
    injury claims, by model, 38, 183–84
    insurance costs, by model, 177
    security concerns, 24
Plymouth
    injury claims, by model, 180, 181, 182, 186
    insurance costs, by model, 170, 177
Plymouth Voyager, 26, 56, 177, 186
Pond, Jonathan, 140
Pontiac
    crash test results, by model, 190, 191, 192
    injury claims, by model, 180–81, 182, 183,
        186
    insurance costs, by model, 170, 172, 173,
        174, 177
Pontiac Firebird, 34, 42, 172, 173, 183
Pontiac Grand Prix, 36, 172, 180, 182, 191
Pontiac Sunbird, 36, 181, 182
Pontiac Trans Sport, 35, 177, 186, 192
Pre-owned cars. *See* Used cars
Price/Costco, 94
Prices
    car-buying services, 88, 90–96
    deal negotiation, 69–75, 123–33, 150–51,
        163, 164
    by model categories, 10–17
    of new cars, 1, 43–44, 64–75, 138
    one-price dealers, 72–73, 88, 89–90,
        97–102, 117
    rebates, 12, 26, 44, 66, 68, 69, 81–82, 83
    research sources, 66–68
    of used cars, 138, 144–45, 150–51
    value-pricing plans, 73, 101–2

Prodigy (on-line service), 68
Purchase options (leasing), 113–14, 168

Rebates, 69
  financing reduction and, 81–82, 83
  research sources, 66, 68
  on slow-selling models, 12, 26, 44
  See also Dealer incentives
Record keeping, 153, 155–56, 160, 164
Rental companies, 75
Repairs
  dealer servicing, 116–22, 148, 155
  service department ratings, 119–20
  vehicle selection and, 10, 56–57
Resale value, 10
Residual value, 46, 104, 106, 109, 110, 168
Road and Track (magazine), 68
Rossi, Kathy, 9–10
Rust, warranties against, 160
Rustproofing, 136–37

Saab
  crash test results, by model, 191
  injury claims, by model, 183, 188
  insurance costs, by model, 173, 174, 175
  new-car warranties, 160
Saab 900, 41, 173, 174, 175, 183, 191
Safety issues, 30–38
  air bags, 31–32, 38
  child safety seats, 32
  crash test results, 33–35, 189–92
  devices available, 38
  injury claims, 35–38, 179–88
  sport utility vehicles and, 27
  See also Car theft; Security concerns
Sales tax, 53, 60
Sam's Club, 94
Saturn
  consumer satisfaction, 98–99, 122
  crash test results, by model, 190
  dealer markup, 72–73
  injury claims, by model, 181, 182, 187
  insurance costs, by model, 170
  one-price shopping and, 98–99, 147
  residual value and, 104
  used-car leasing, 115
  used-car warranties, 49, 141, 148
Saturn SC, 36, 170

Saturn SL, 34, 170
Saturn SW, 18, 41, 170, 187
Savings and loan institutions, 76
Schoonmaker, Alan, 87–88
Seat belts, 38
Security concerns, 24, 39–42
Seger, Bob, 17
Selection. *See* Vehicle selection
Service departments (dealer), 116–22, 148, 155
Shows, auto, 73–74
Side-impact bags, 32
Skopec, Eric, 128, 130
Small cars
  category overview, 10–11
  crash test results, by model, 34, 189–90
  injury claims, by model, 36, 181, 182–83, 187
  insurance costs, by model, 169–70
Software products, leasing analysis, 107–8
Sound systems, 25
Spinella, Art, 108, 114–15
Sport utility vehicles (SUVs), 27–28
  business tax deductions and, 51–52
  cargo space, 22
  category overview, 16
  crash test results, by model, 35, 191–92
  gas mileage, 25
  injury claims, by model, 37, 185–86
  insurance costs, by model, 175–76
  maintenance costs, 56
  residual value and, 104
  safety issues, 27
  security concerns, 24
  as used cars, 49
Sporty cars
  category overview, 14–15
  injury claims, by model, 183
Station cars, 24
Station wagons
  cargo space, 22
  injury claims, by model, 186–87
  vehicle selection and, 18
Sticker price. *See* Manufacturer's suggested retail price
Stolen cars. *See* Car theft
Strategic Research and Consulting Group, 47, 48
Subaru
  consumer satisfaction, 122
  crash test results, by model, 190

injury claims, by model, 181, 183, 187
insurance costs, by model, 172, 173, 175
Subaru Impreza, 41, 172, 181, 190
Subaru Legacy Outback, 18
Subcompact cars
  crash test results, 34
  See also Small cars
Subsidized leases, 12, 44, 67, 103, 104, 106
Superstores (automobile), 43, 50, 99, 141,
  145–46
SUVs. *See* Sport utility vehicles
Suzuki Sidekick, 176, 186

Taxes
  business deductions, 51–52
  home-equity loans and, 77
  luxury, 140
  sales, 53, 60
Test drives, 74–75
Theft. *See* Car theft
Toyota
  anticorrosion warranties, 136
  consumer satisfaction, 122
  crash test results, by model, 190, 191, 192
  injury claims, by model, 181, 182, 183, 184,
    185, 186, 187
  insurance costs, by model, 170, 172, 173,
    174, 176, 177
  Internet address, 68
  residual value and, 104
  See also Lexus
Toyota Camry, 25, 34, 40, 172, 173, 181, 187,
  190, 191
Toyota Corolla, 18, 170, 172, 181, 187,
  190
Toyota 4-Runner, 37, 176, 185, 192
Toyota Land Cruiser, 37, 40, 176, 185
Toyota Paseo, 36, 170, 183
Toyota Pickup, 38, 177, 184
Toyota Previa, 37, 177, 186, 192
Toyota Tacoma, 28, 177, 192
Toyota Tercel, 24, 170, 181, 183, 190
Trade-in value, 58–60
  deal negotiation and, 100–101, 131–32
  depreciation and, 57
  negative equity, 62
  used car prices and, 150
Transportation fees. *See* Freight charges

Trucks
  business tax deductions, 51–52
  See also Pickup trucks
Trunk space. *See* Cargo space

Upside down (equity position), 62, 166
Used cars
  buying tips, 138–53
  car size considerations, 18–19
  commuting needs and, 24
  deal negotiation, 150–51, 153
  depreciation as cost factor, 152
  financing of, 82–83, 139
  formerly leased cars sold as, 43
  illegal practices, 142
  inspection of, 149
  insurance and, 49
  leasing of, 49–50, 114–15
  "lemons," 154, 155, 157
  maintenance considerations, 50
  manufacturer certification programs, 49,
    115, 141, 148
  needs assessment, 48–50, 139–40, 141,
    142
  one-price selling and, 99–100, 145, 147
  price research, 144–45
  problem warning signs, 151
  ratings of, 143
  sources for, 43, 50, 141, 145–49
  trading-in versus selling, 59–60, 100–101,
    131–32
  value determination, 58–59
  warranties, 24, 49, 57, 141, 148, 155, 160,
    164

Value-pricing plans, 73, 101–2
Vehicle selection
  buying vs. leasing, 43–52
  cost considerations, 10, 53–63, 138
  deal negotiation, 69–75, 123–33, 150–51,
    153, 162–64
  "lemon" avoidance, 154–58, 164
  maintenance as factor, 10, 56, 116–22
  model categories, 10–17
  needs assessment, 8–10, 17–19, 20–29,
    44–50, 139–40, 141, 142
  new versus used, 48–50

(Vehicle selection, continued)
  price determination, 64–75
  purchase add-ons, 133–37
  resale value, 10
  safety issues, 30–38
  test drives, 74–75
  theft and security concerns, 24, 39–42
  trade-ins as factor, 59–60, 100–101
Volkswagen
  anticorrosion warranties, 136
  crash test results, by model, 190, 191
  injury claims, by model, 181
  insurance costs, by model, 170, 172, 173
Volvo
  consumer satisfaction, 122
  crash test results, by model, 191
  injury claims, by model, 181, 188
  insurance costs, by model, 174, 175

  new-car warranties, 160
Volvo 850, 25, 32, 36, 174, 181, 191

Warehouse shopping clubs, 93–94
Warranties
  anticorrosion, 136
  auto brokers and, 95, 157
  coverages, stipulations, 160
  extended, 135, 161, 164
  leasing and, 108
  "lemon" cars and, 155–56
  on new cars, 56–57, 134
  scheduled maintenance and, 116
  on used cars, 24, 49, 57, 141, 148, 155, 160, 164
Women, sport utility vehicles and, 27
World Wide Web. *See* Internet